LETTER TRACING FOR KIDS

AVERY

TRACE MY NAME WORKBOOK

Have our elves create a personalized book
with the name of your choice today!

VISIT US AT:

PERSONALIZETHISBOOK.COM

Cover and page design by Cool Journals Studios - Copyright 2017

About Me

My name is:

Avery

I live in:

For parents

For kids

I am ☐ years old.

Draw you and your family

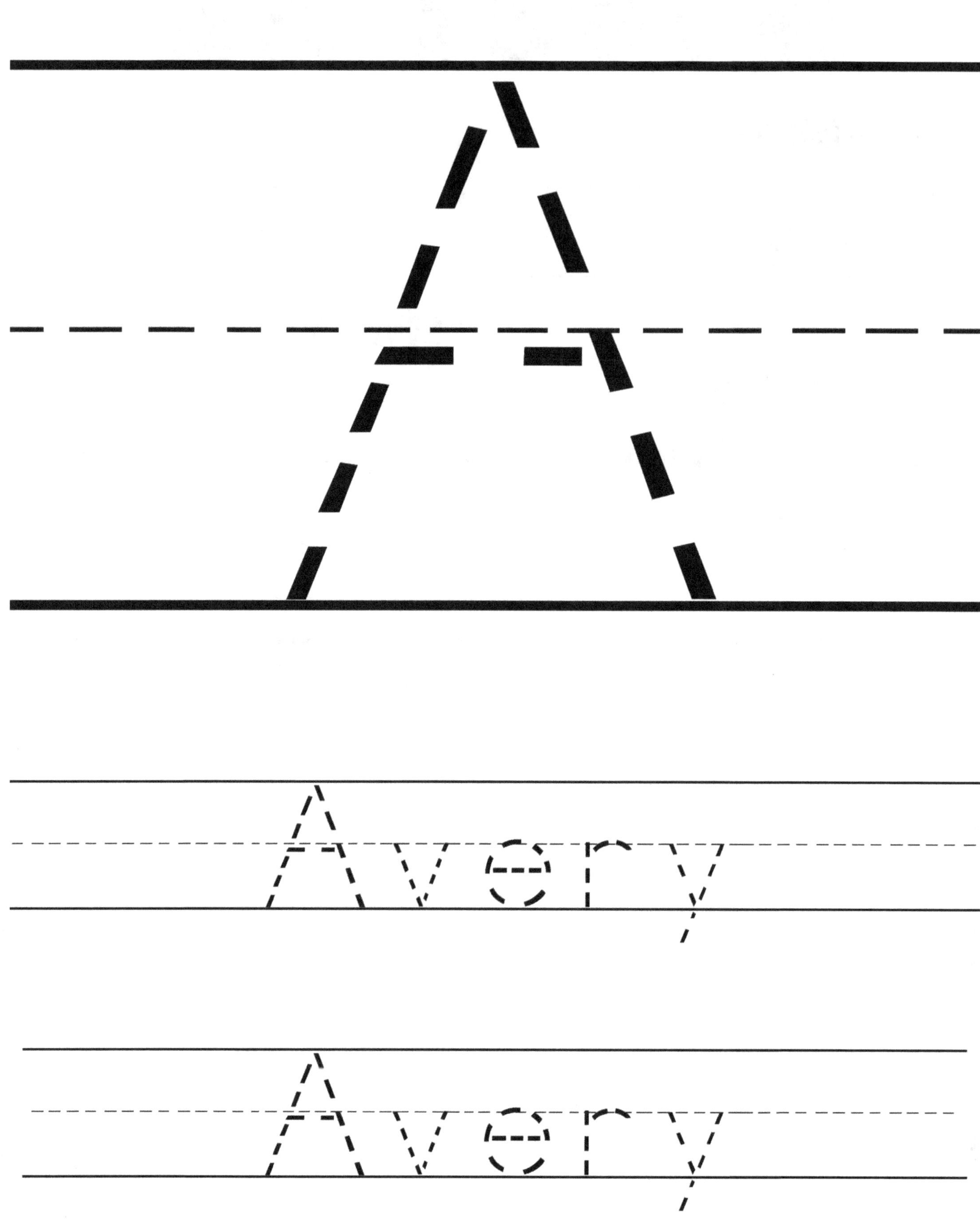

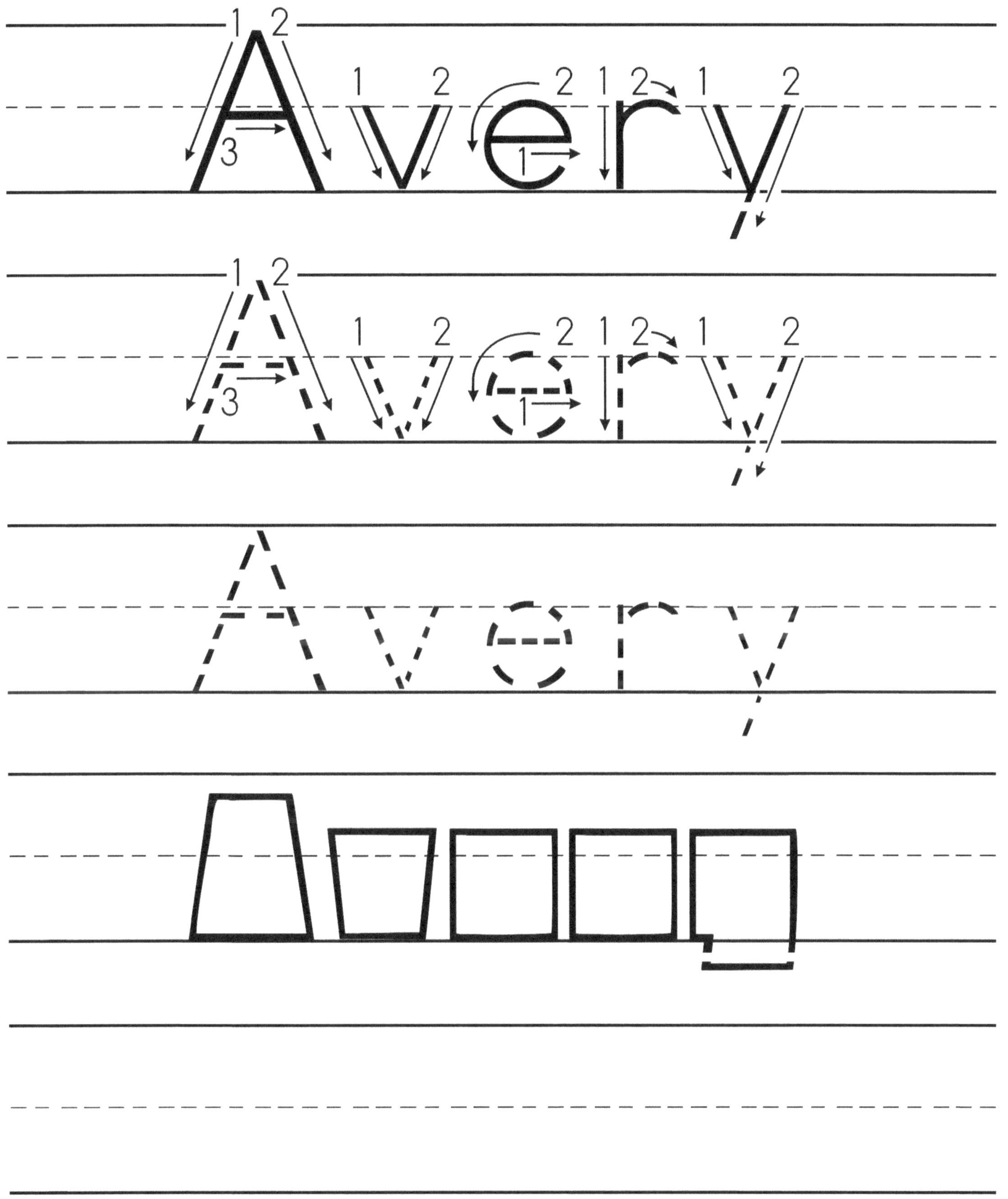

THIS IS HOW I WRITE MY NAME

MY NAME HAS ___ LETTERS

Avery

very

ery

ry

y

Avery

COLOR THE EGGS WITH LETTERS OF OUR NAME WRITE YOUR NAME

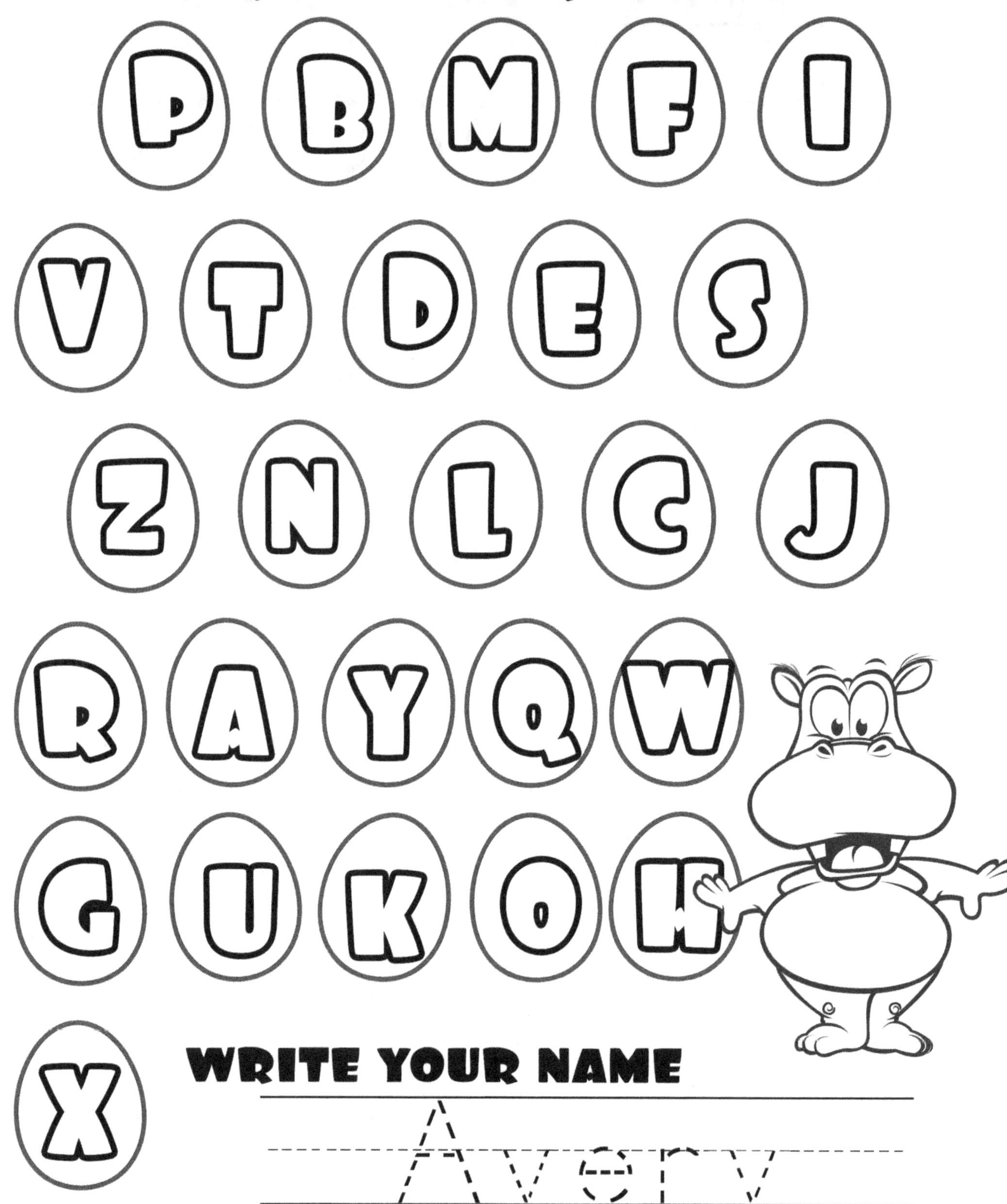

WRITE YOU NAME WITH,

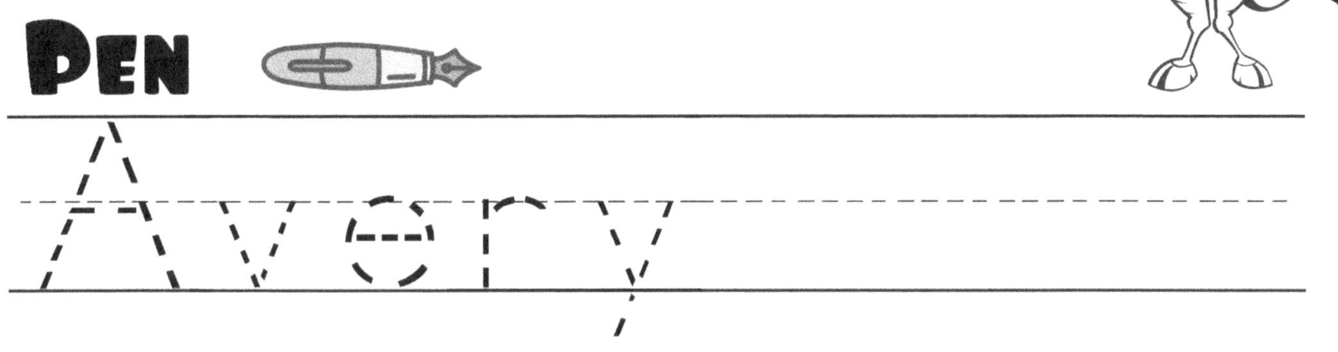

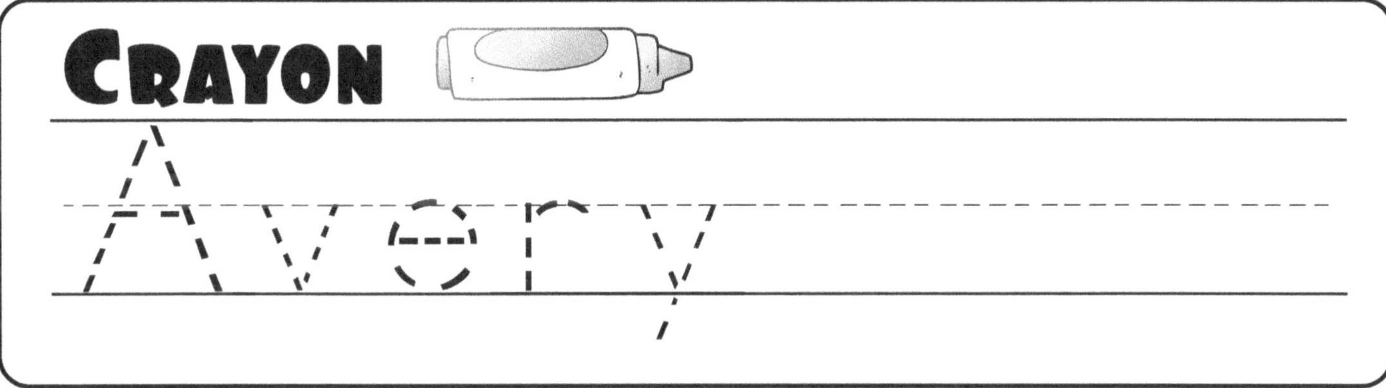

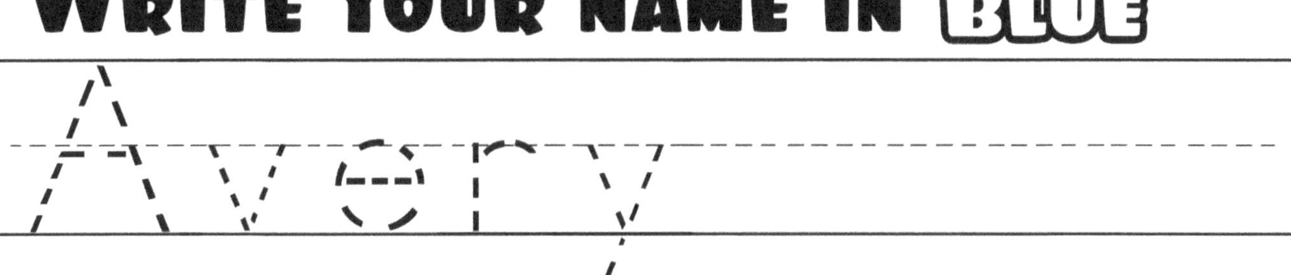

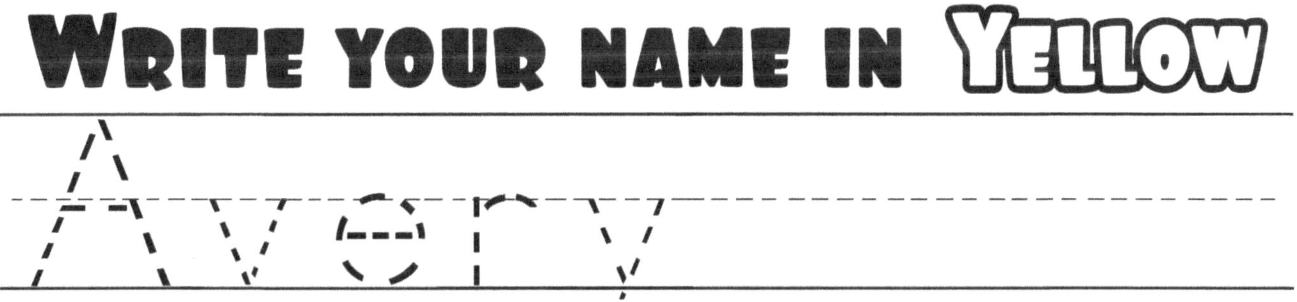

Draw Your Favorite Things

Color

Food

Toy

Animal

MY NAME

<table>
<tr><td>MY NAME
STARTS WITH

_______</td><td>MY NAME
ENDS WITH

_______</td></tr>
</table>

FILL THE LETTERS OF YOUR NAME WHITH DIFFERENT COLORS

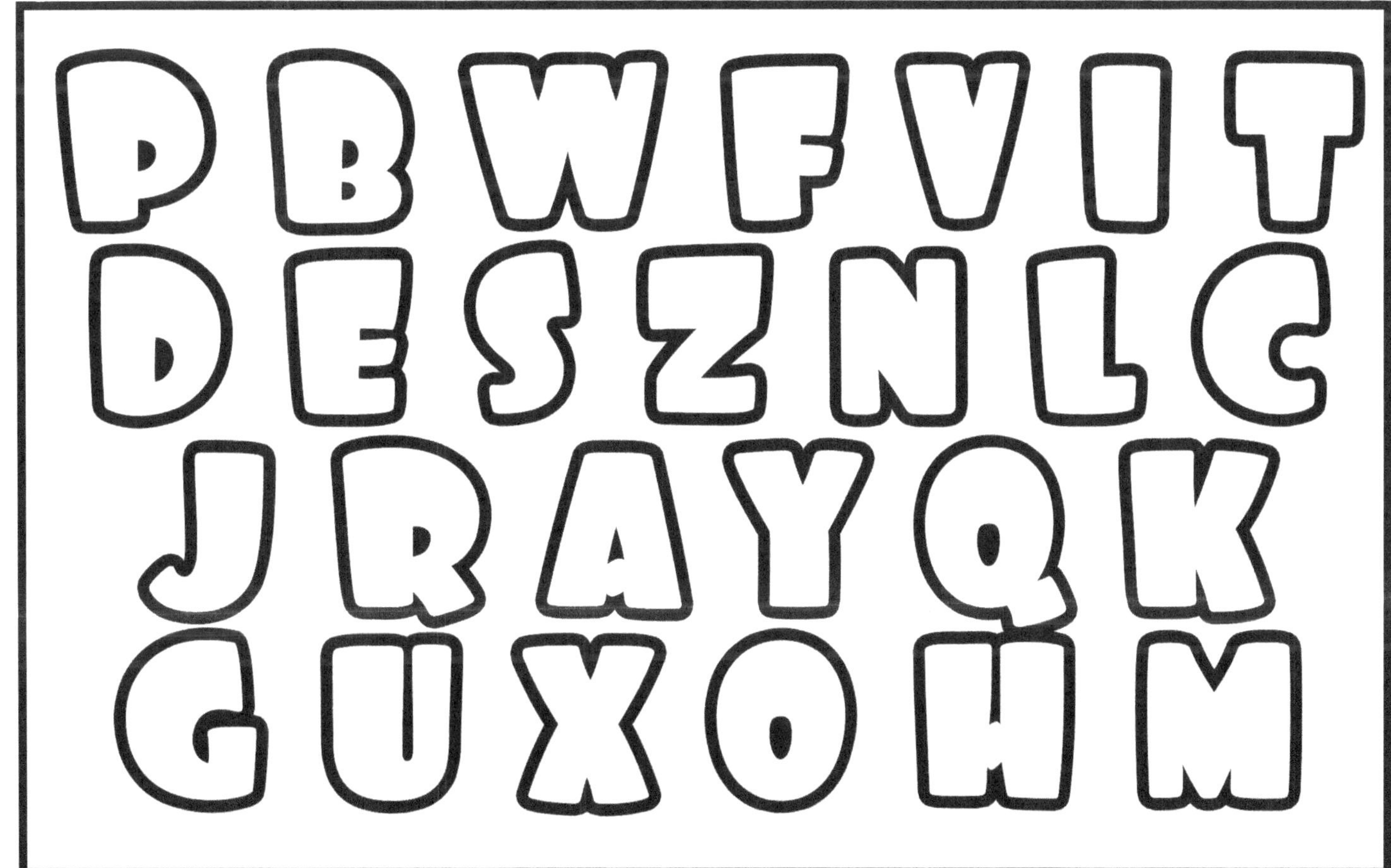

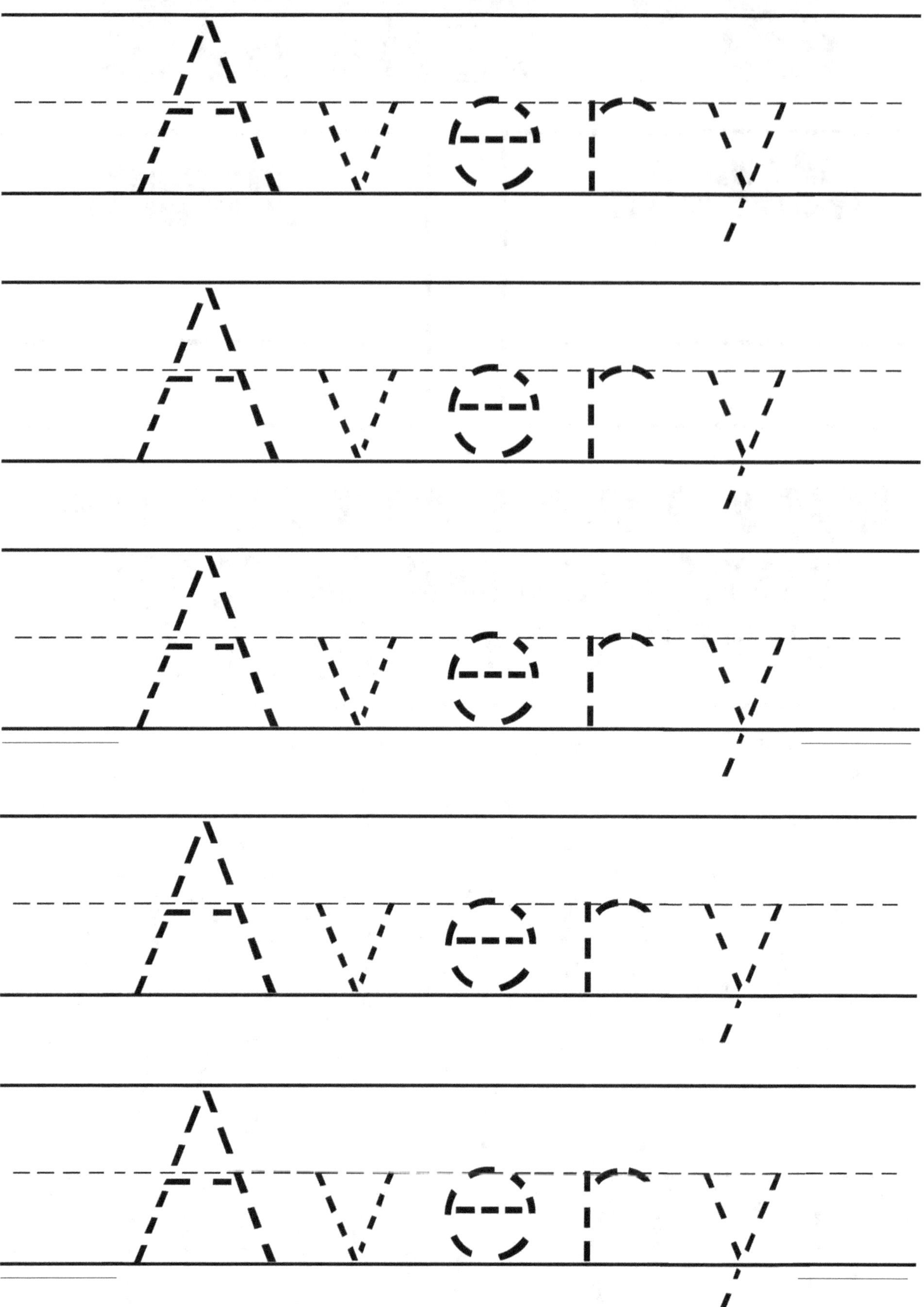

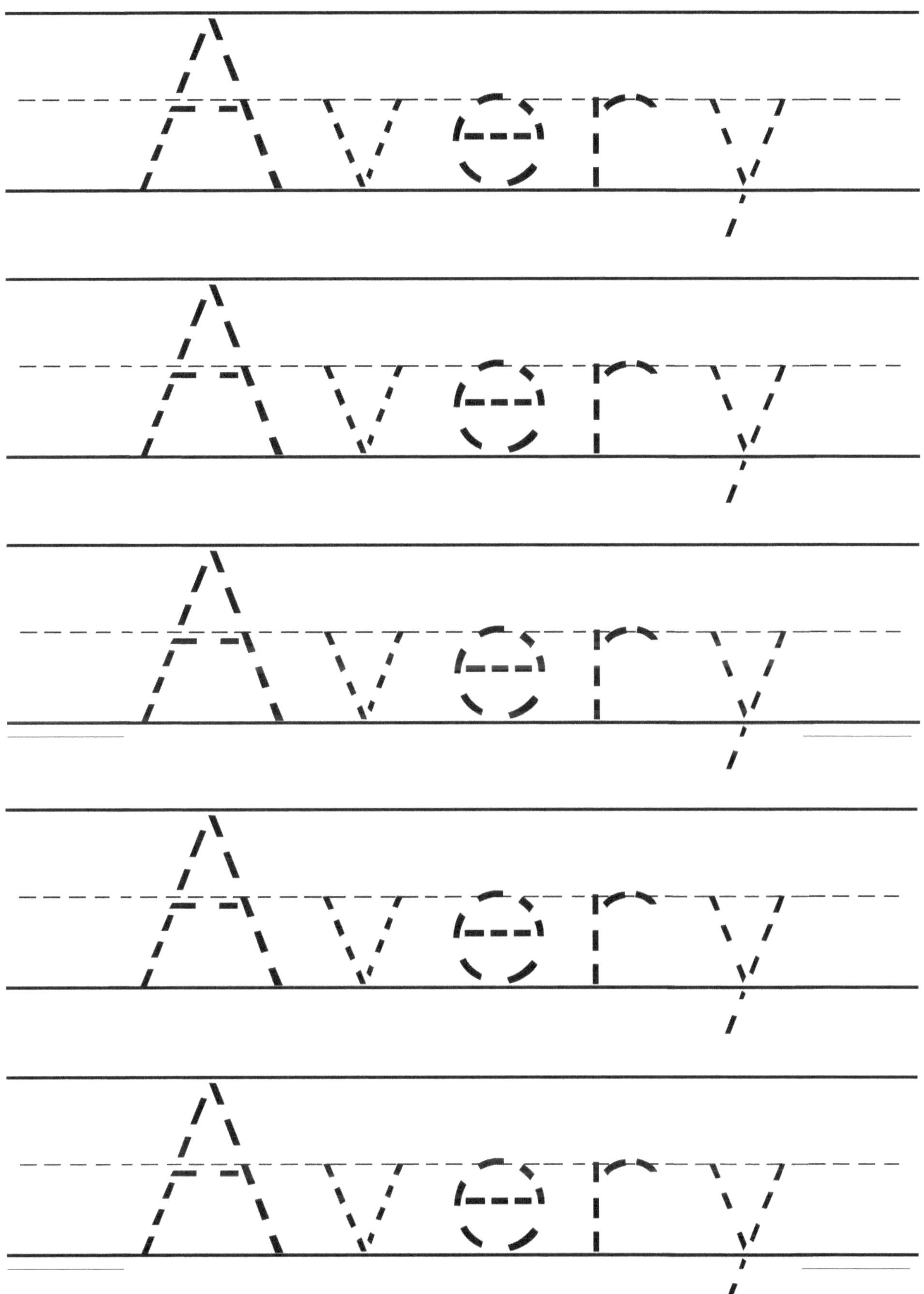

Avery
Avery
Avery
Avery
Avery

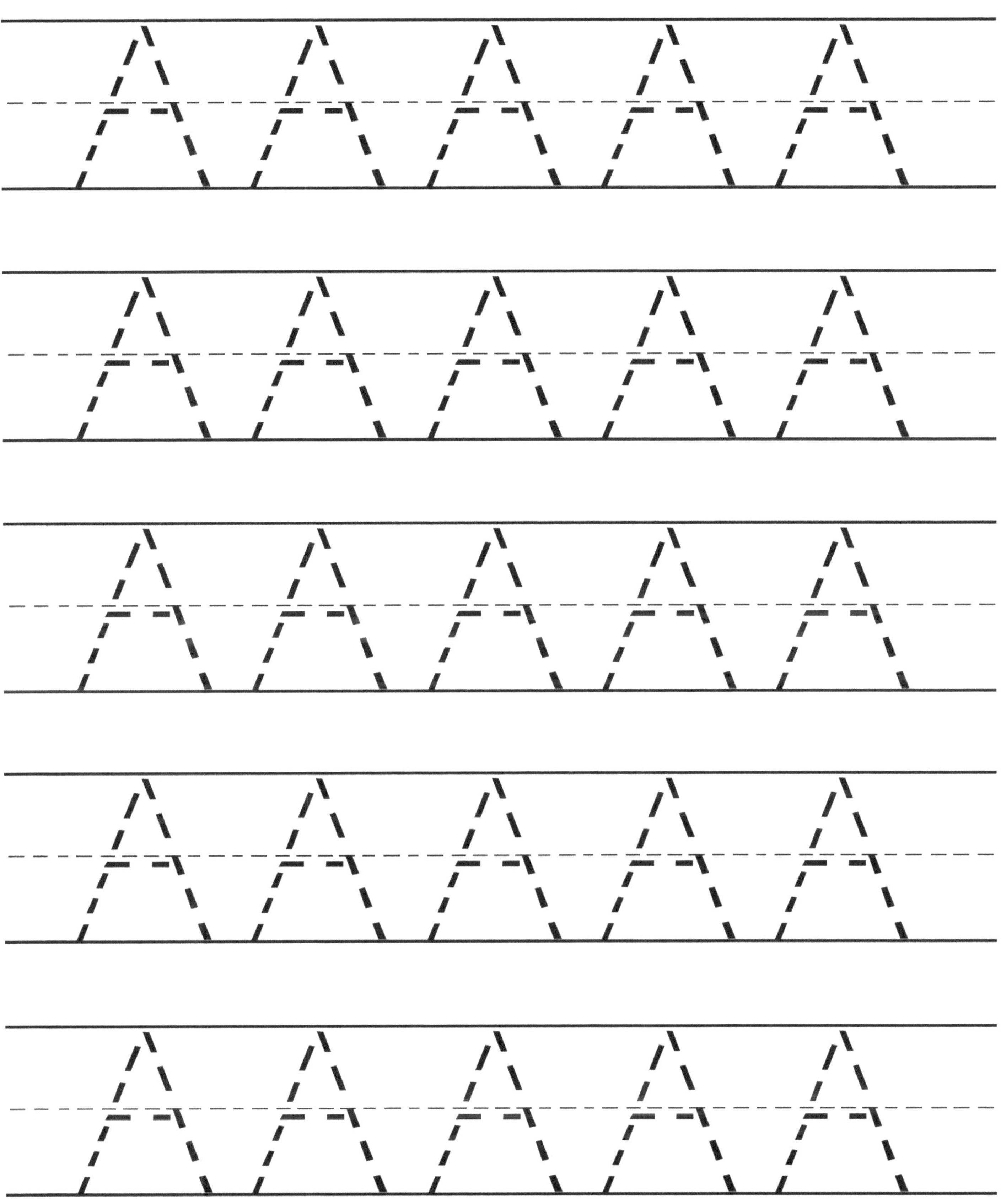

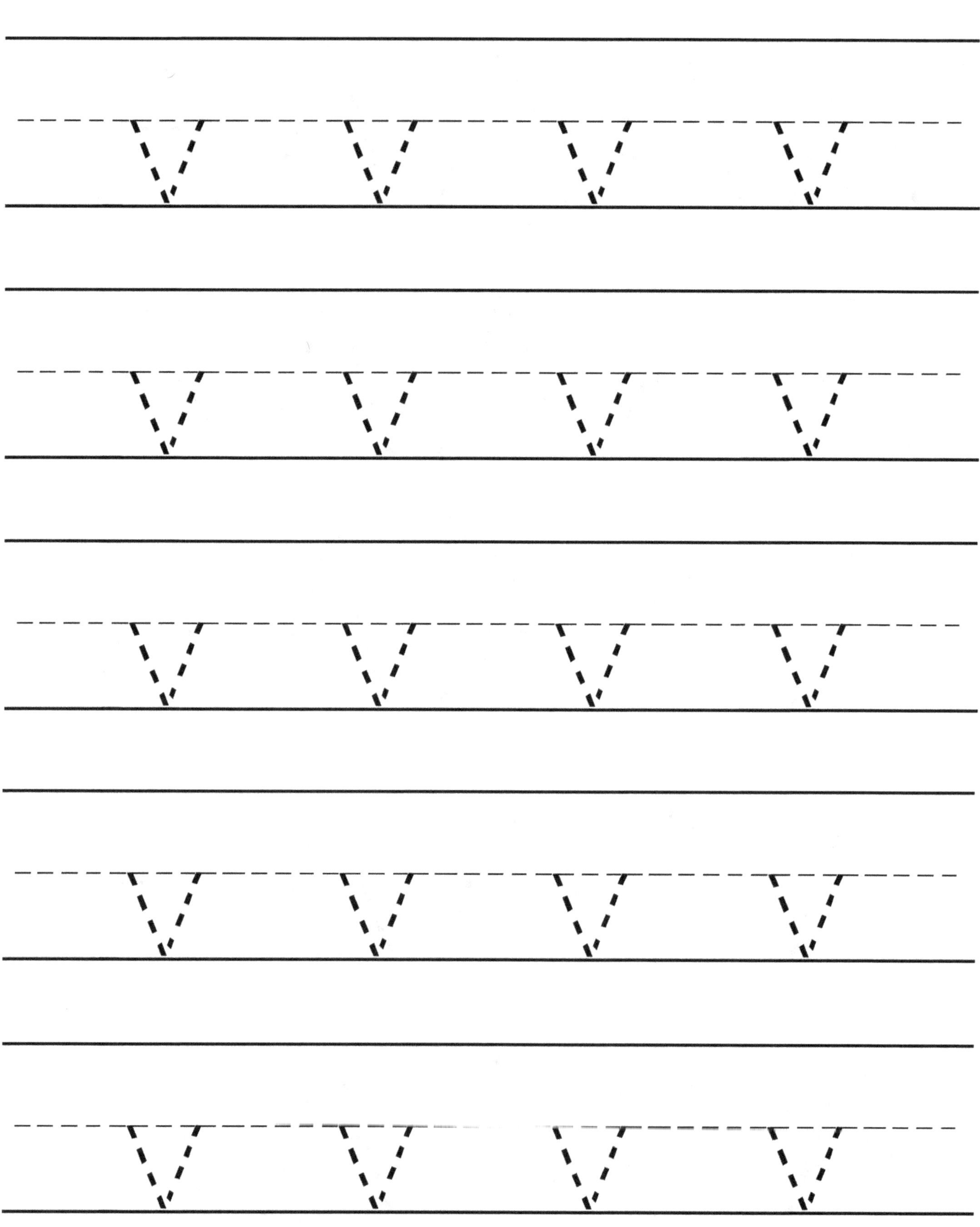

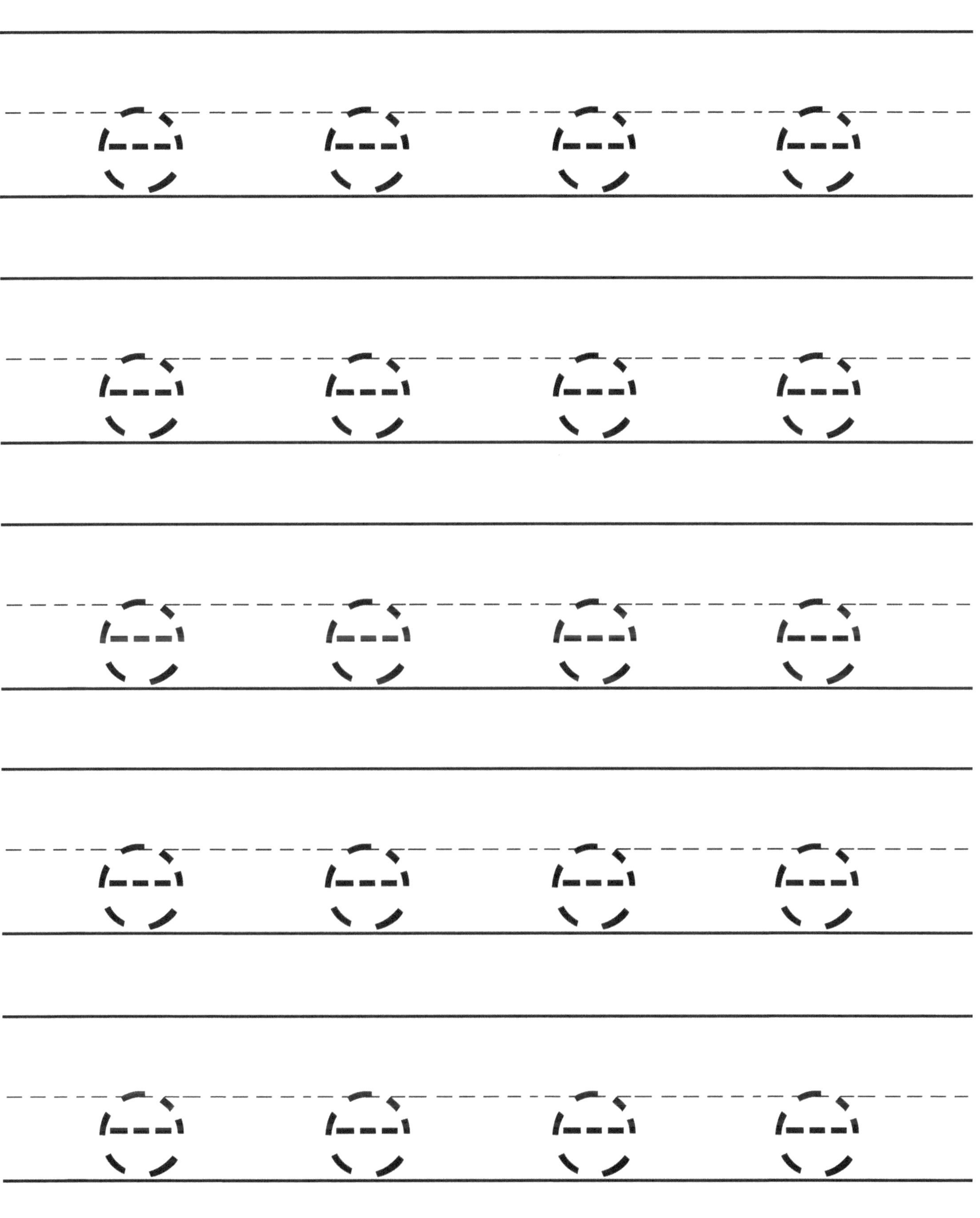

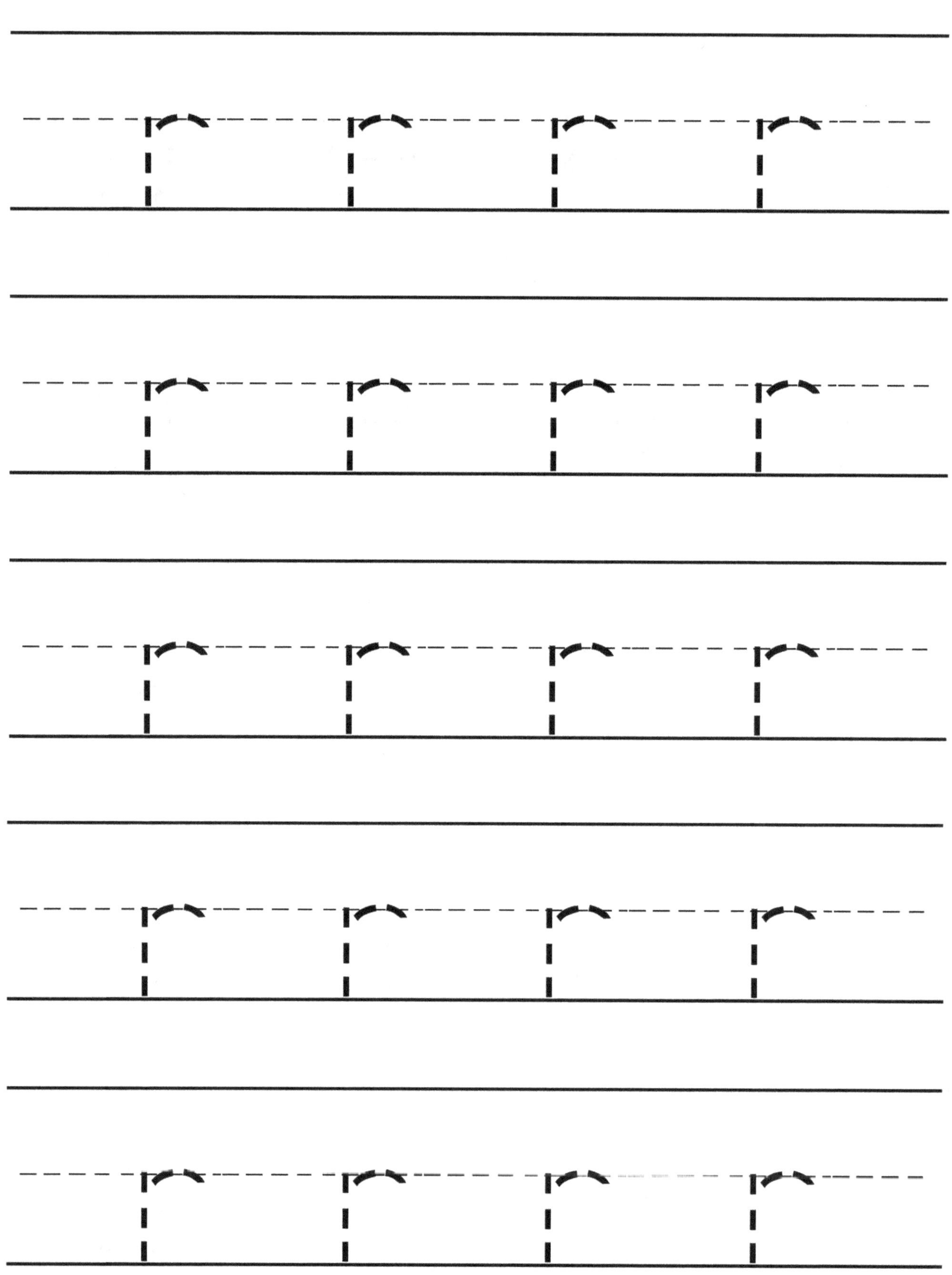

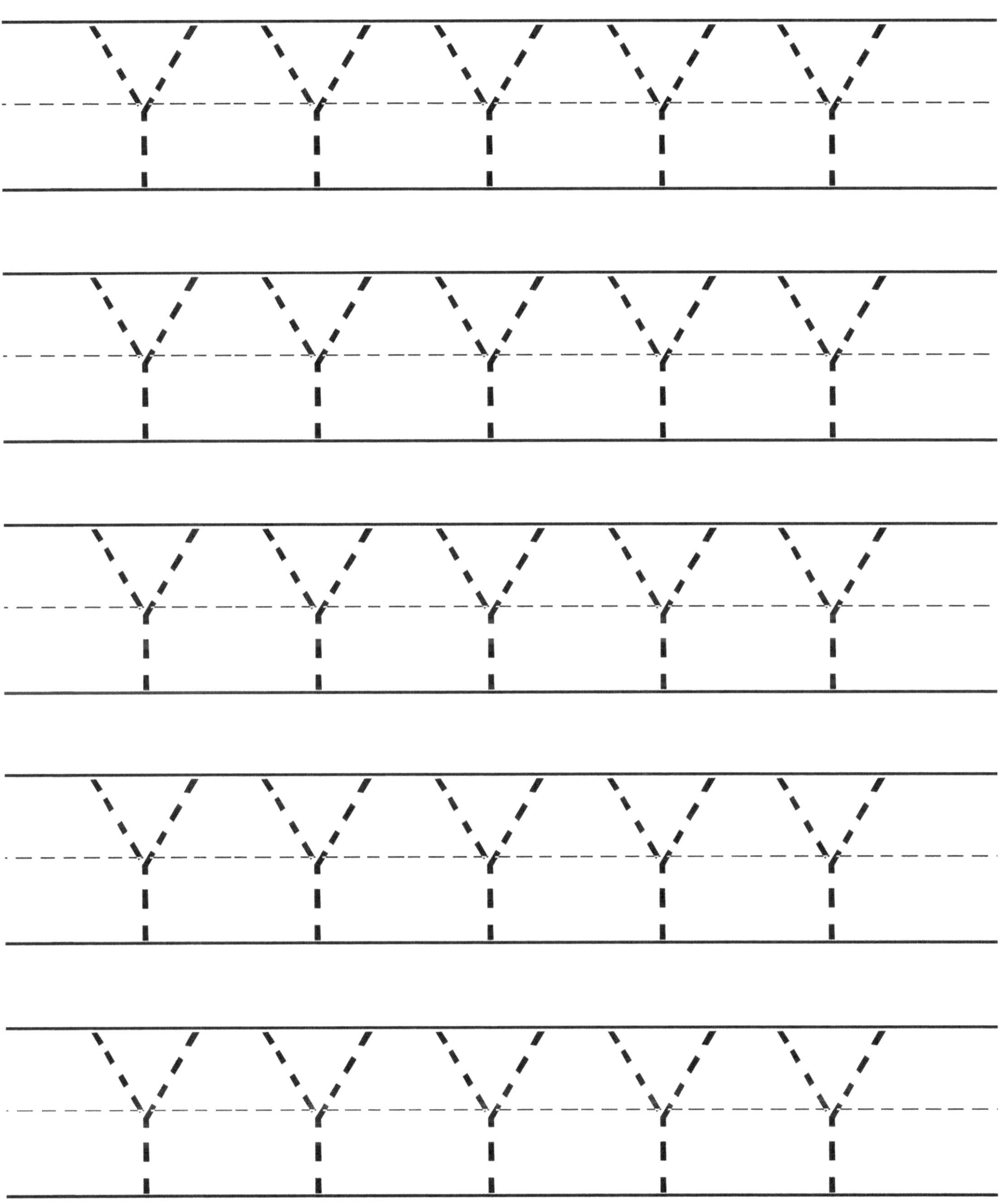

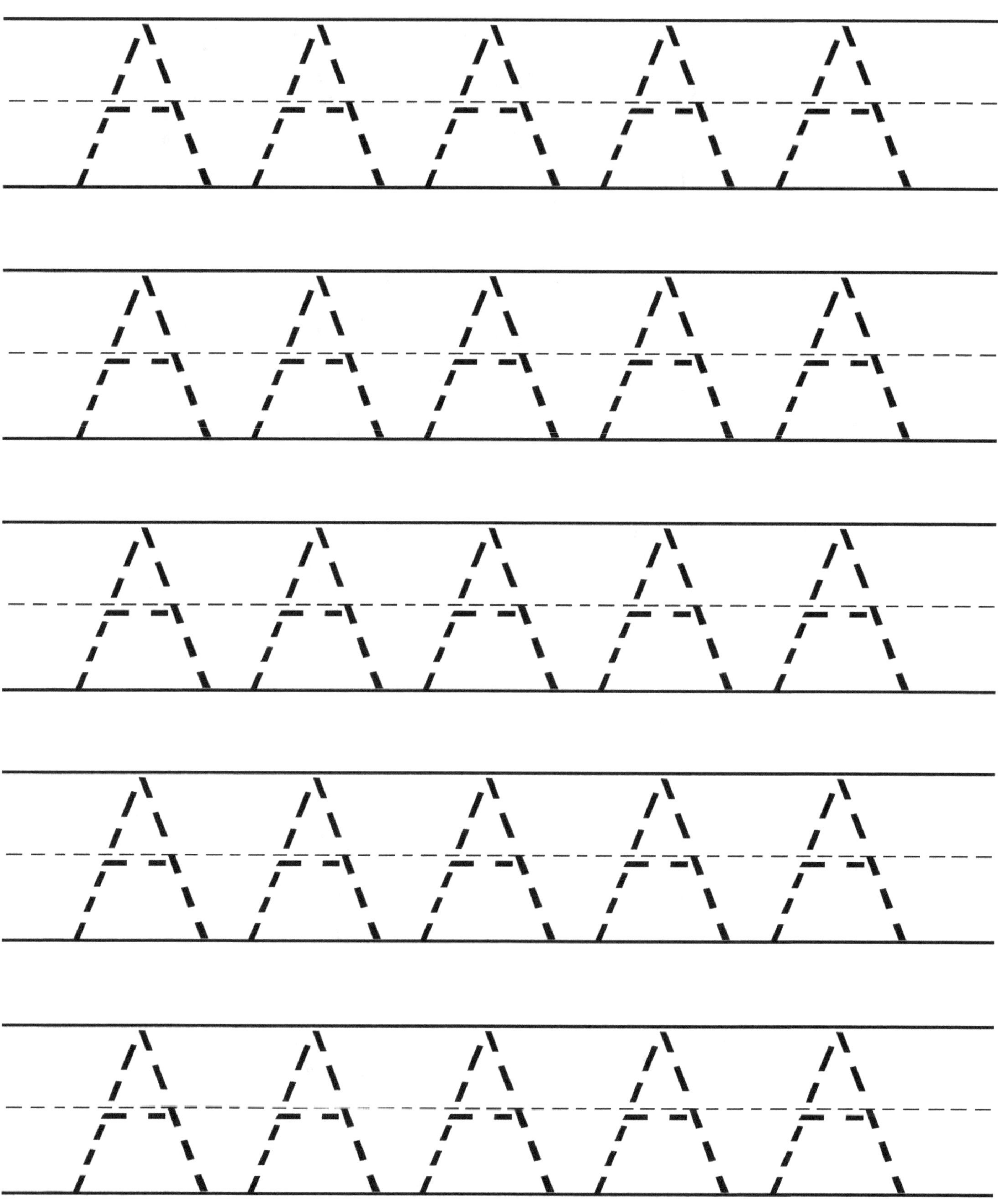

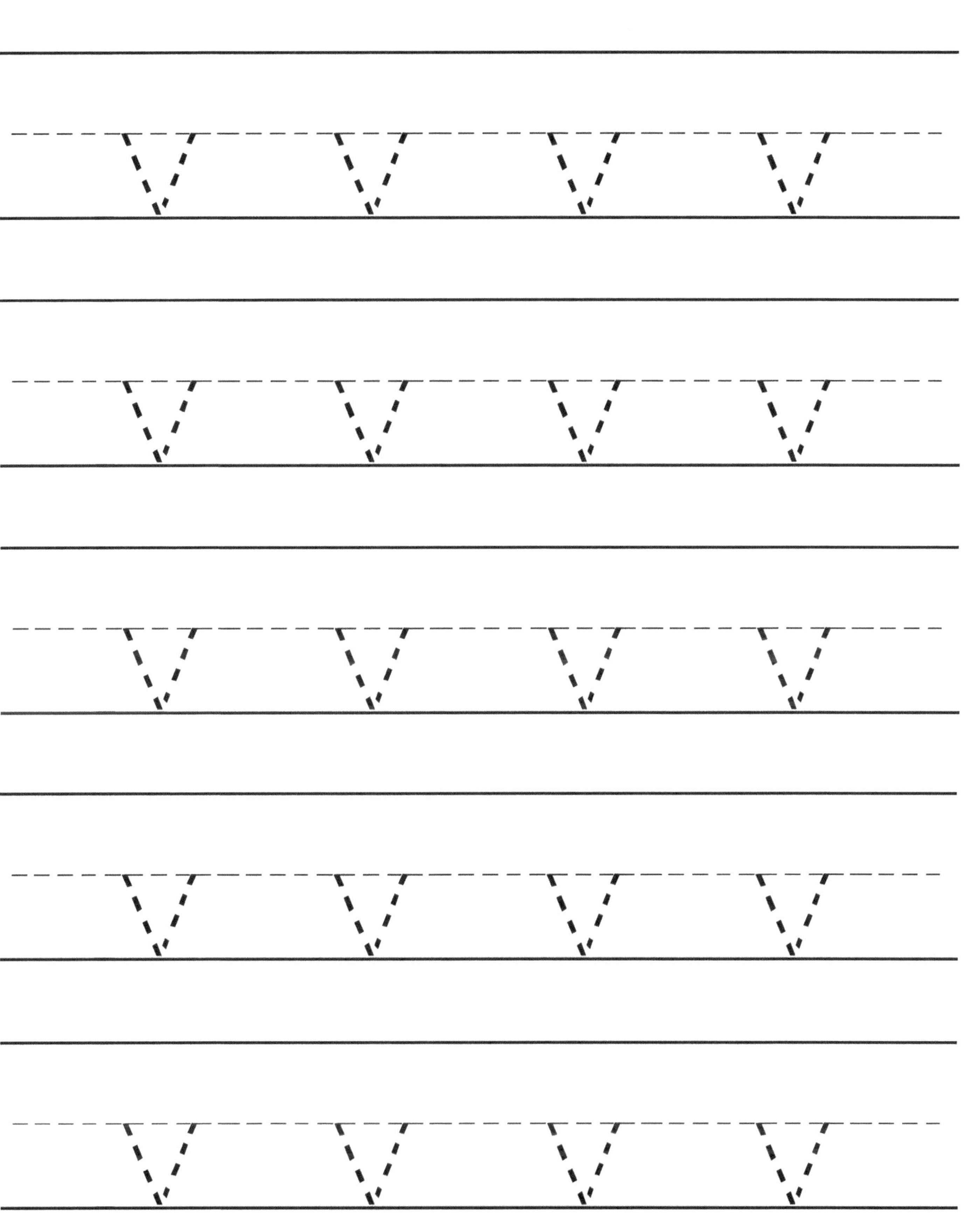

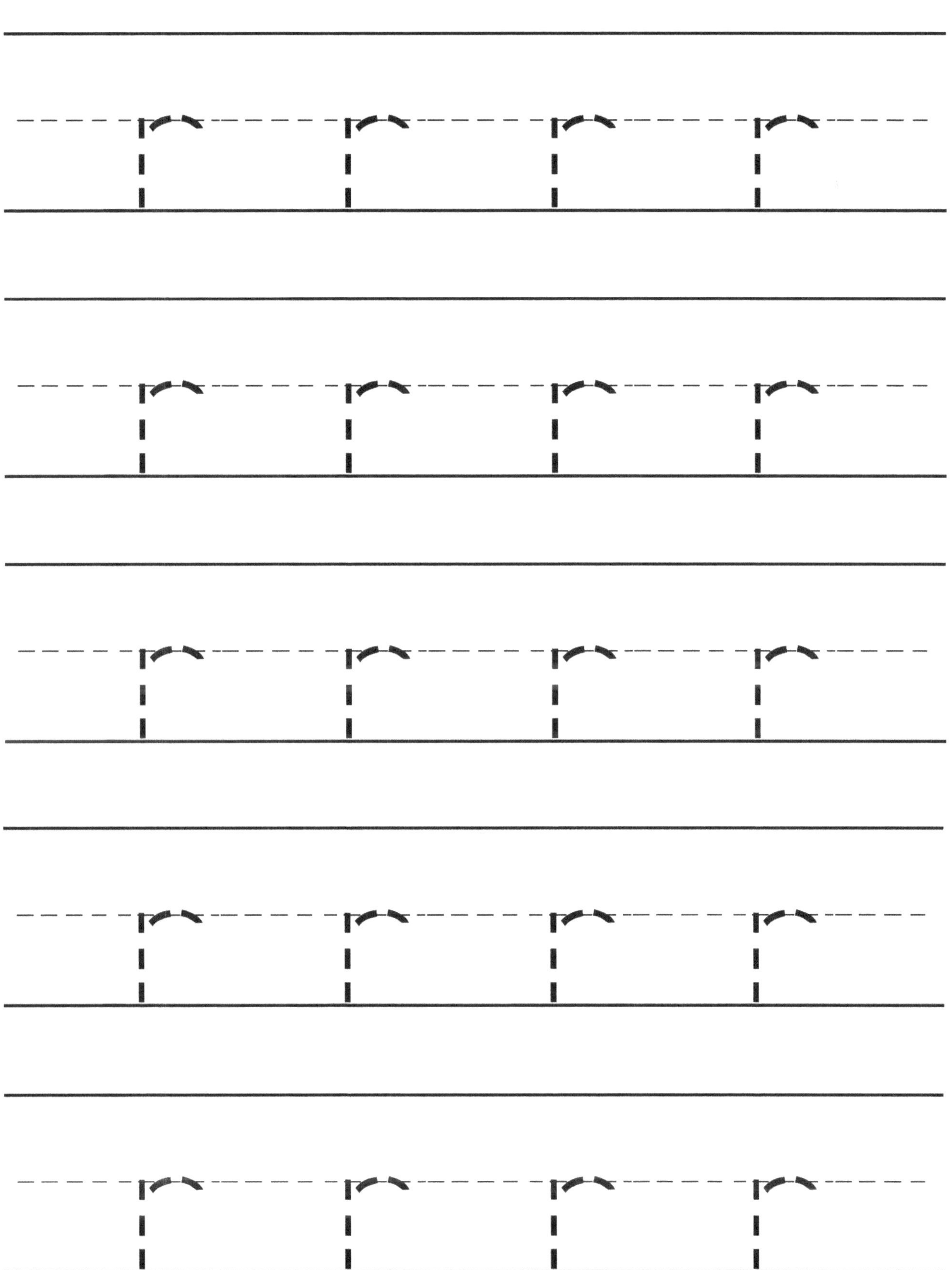

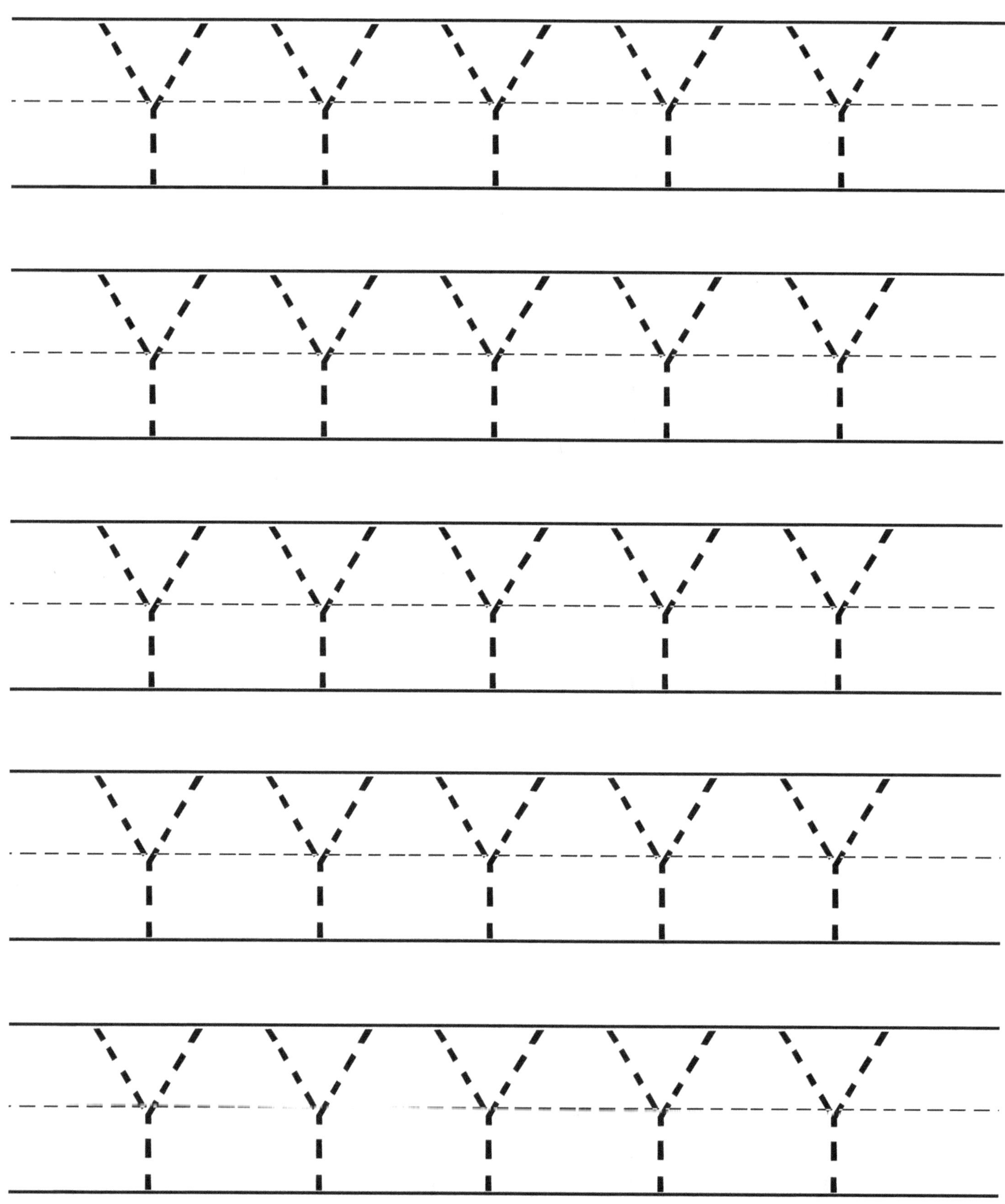

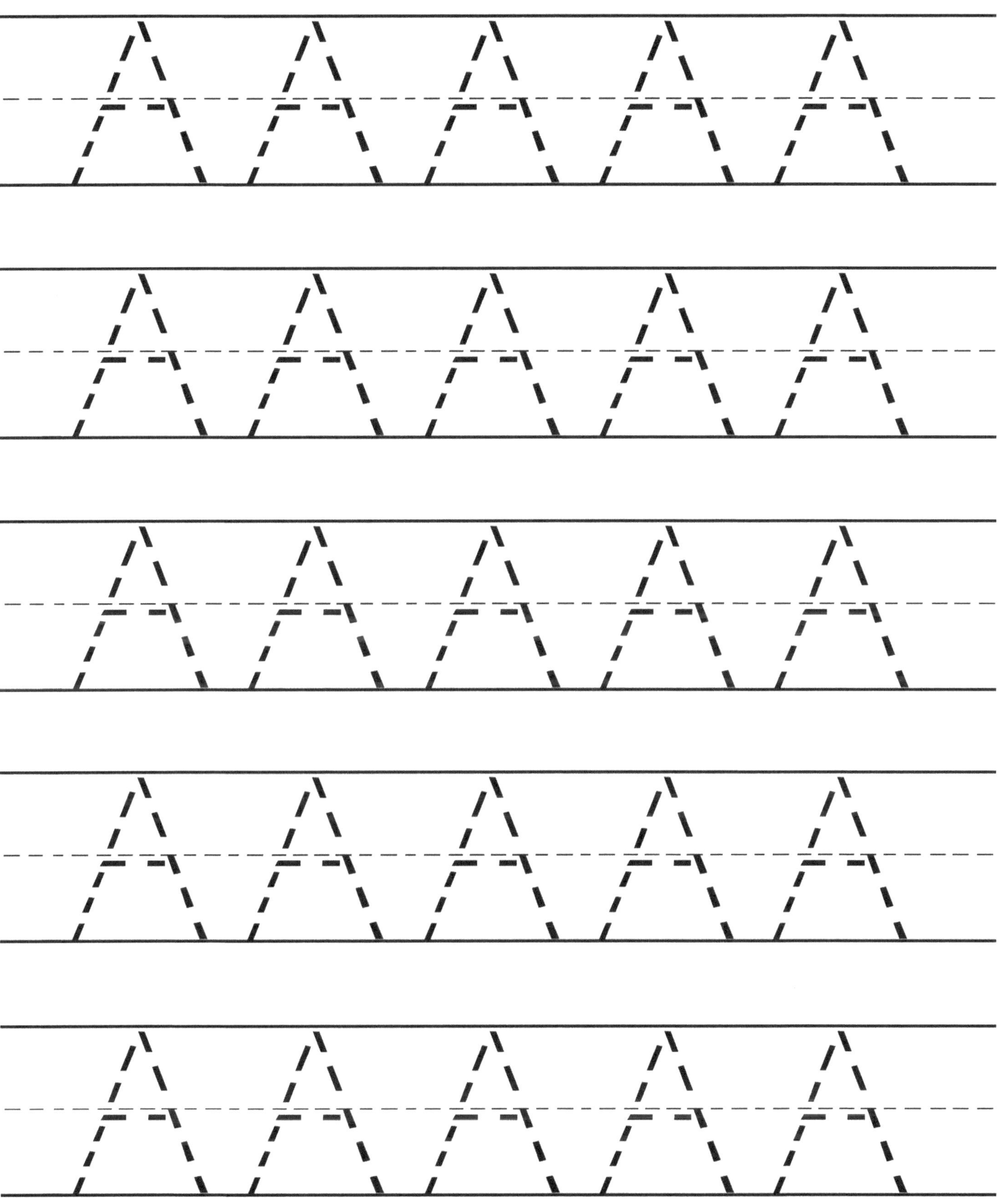

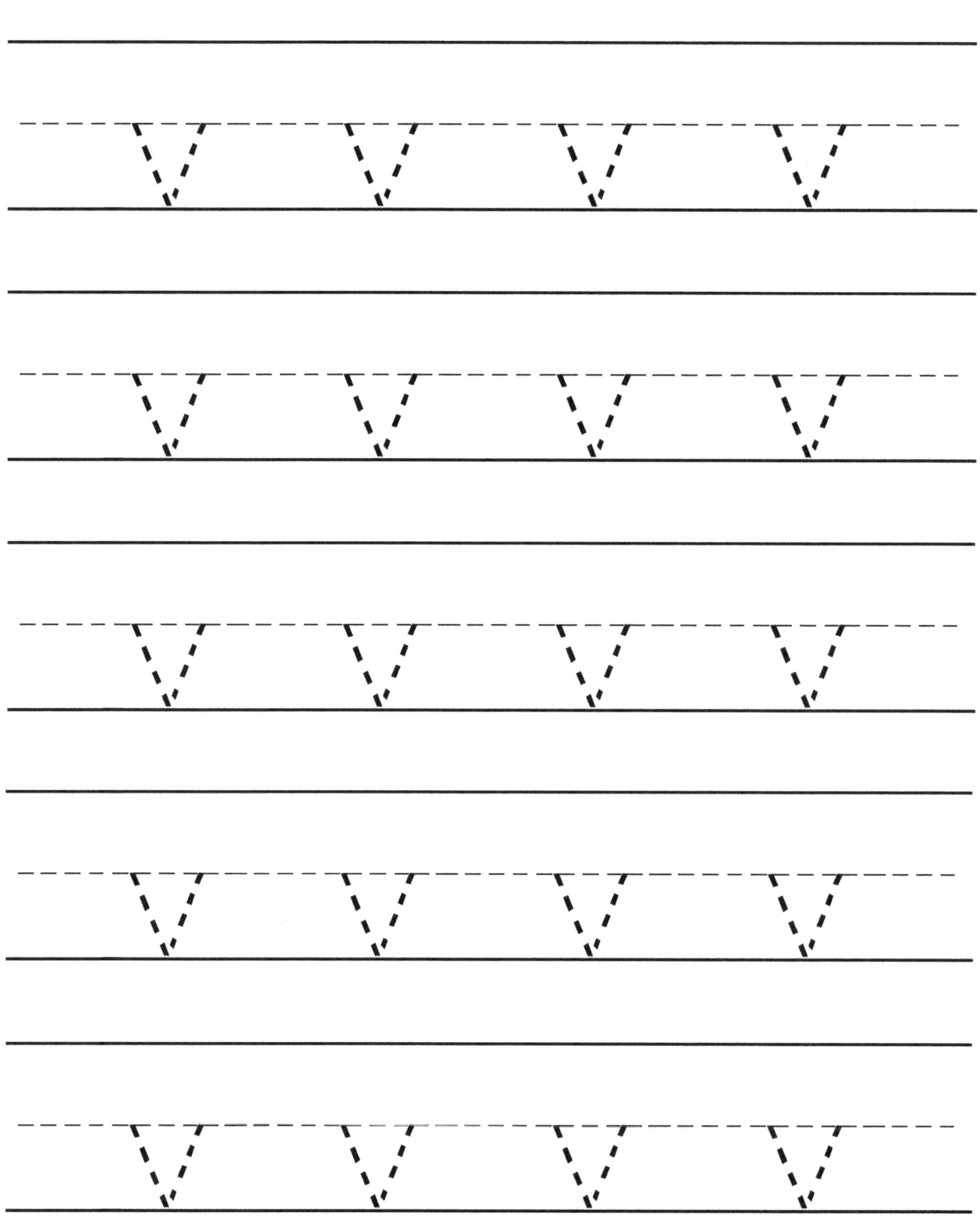

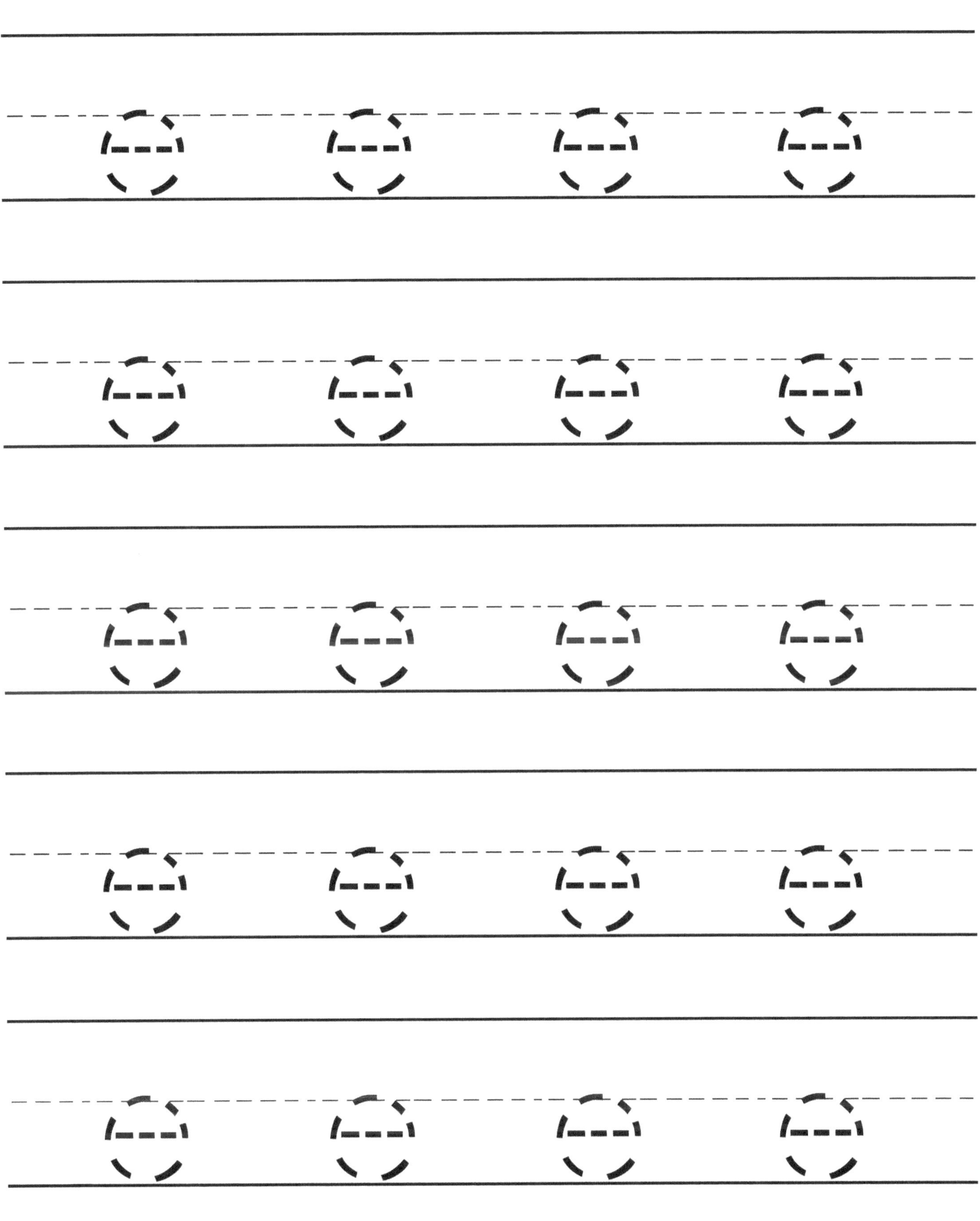

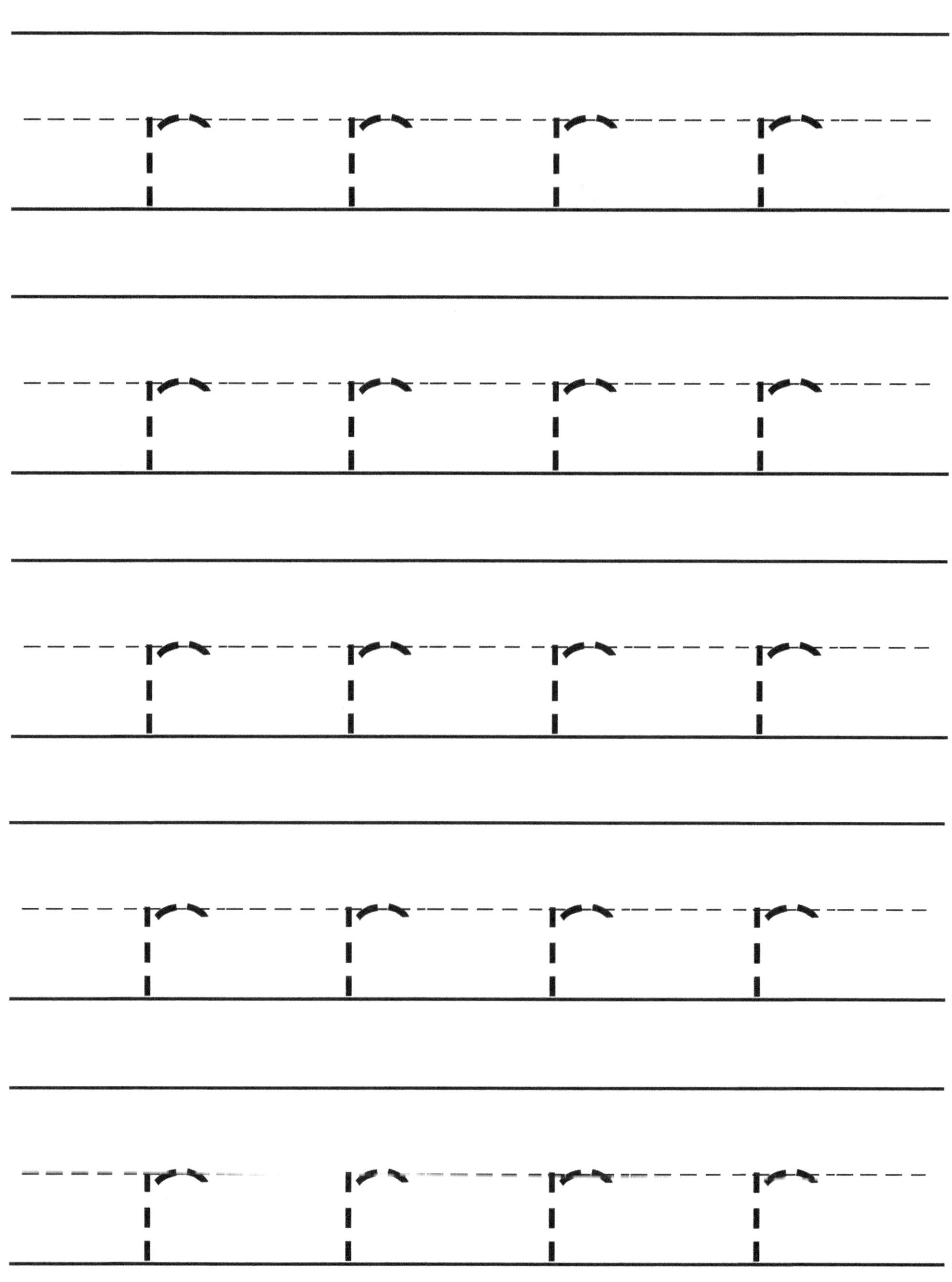

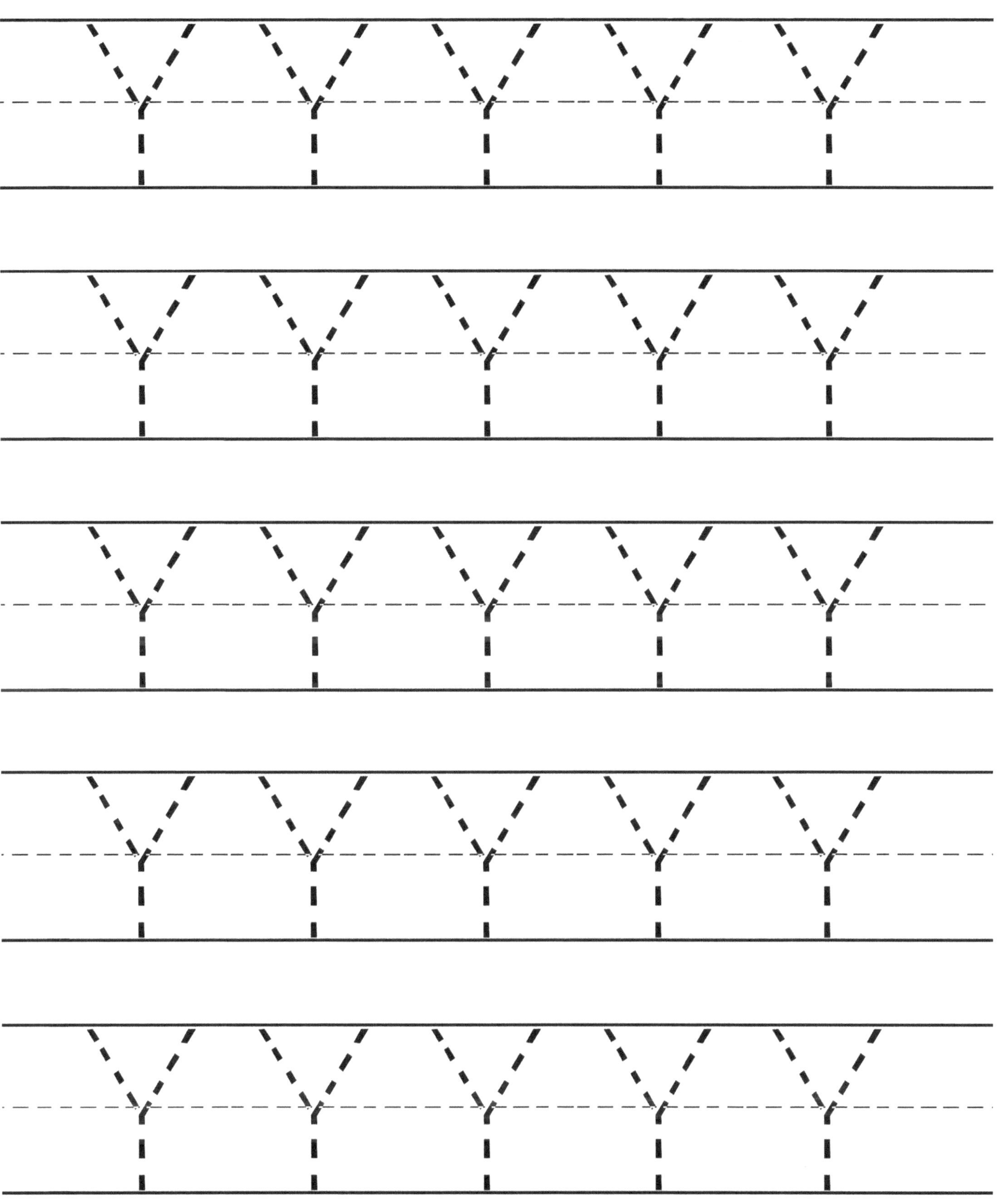

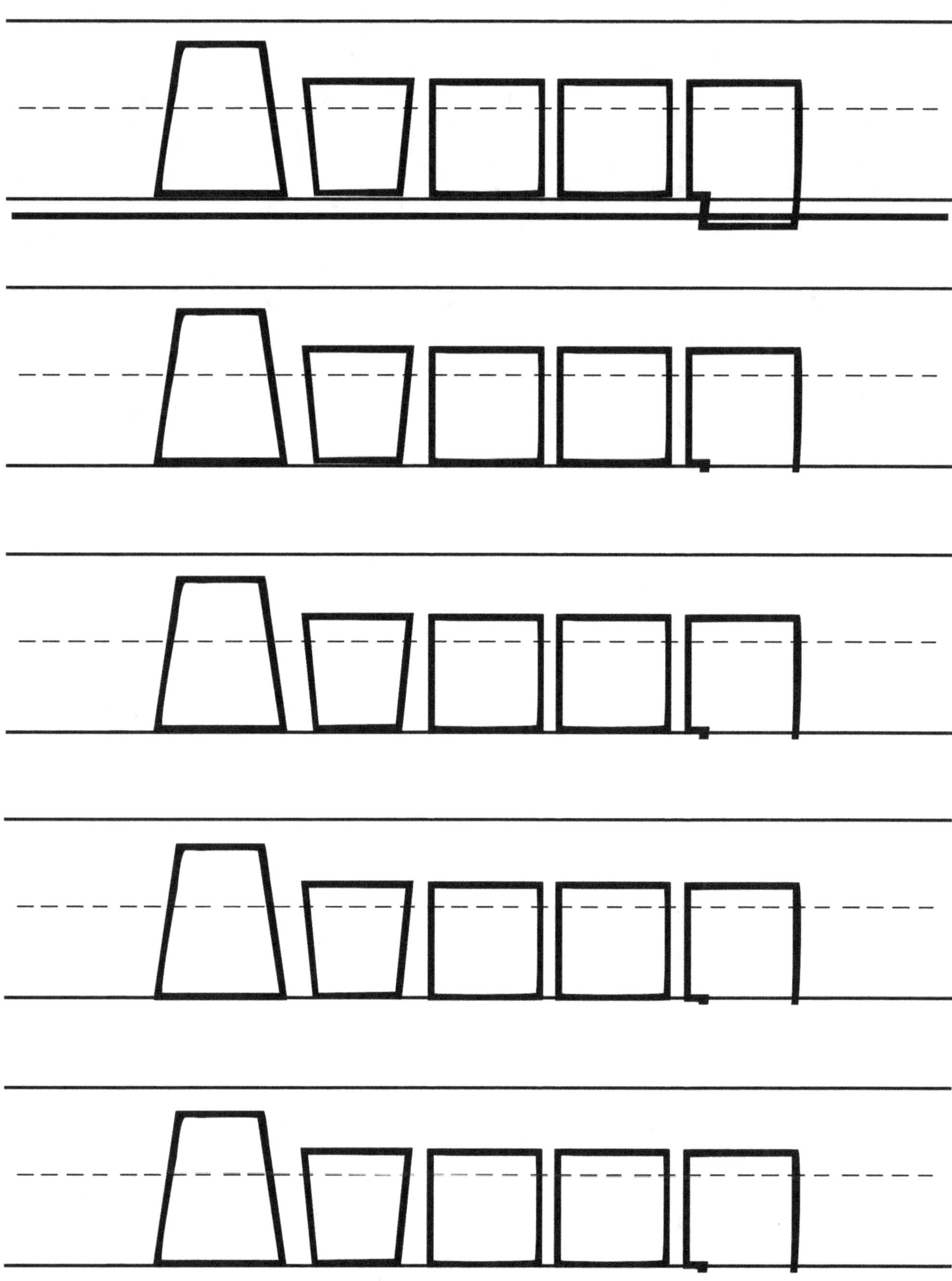

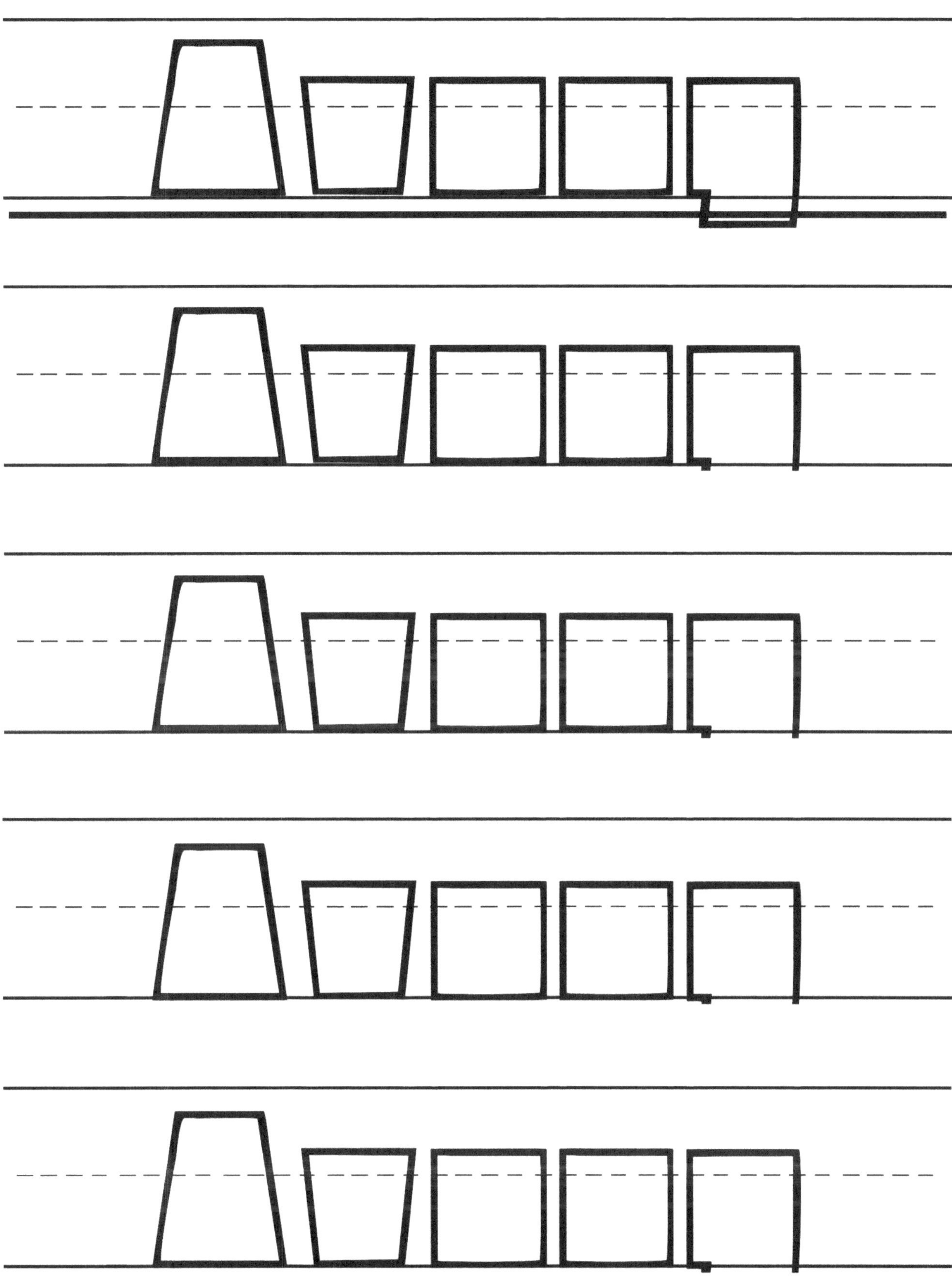

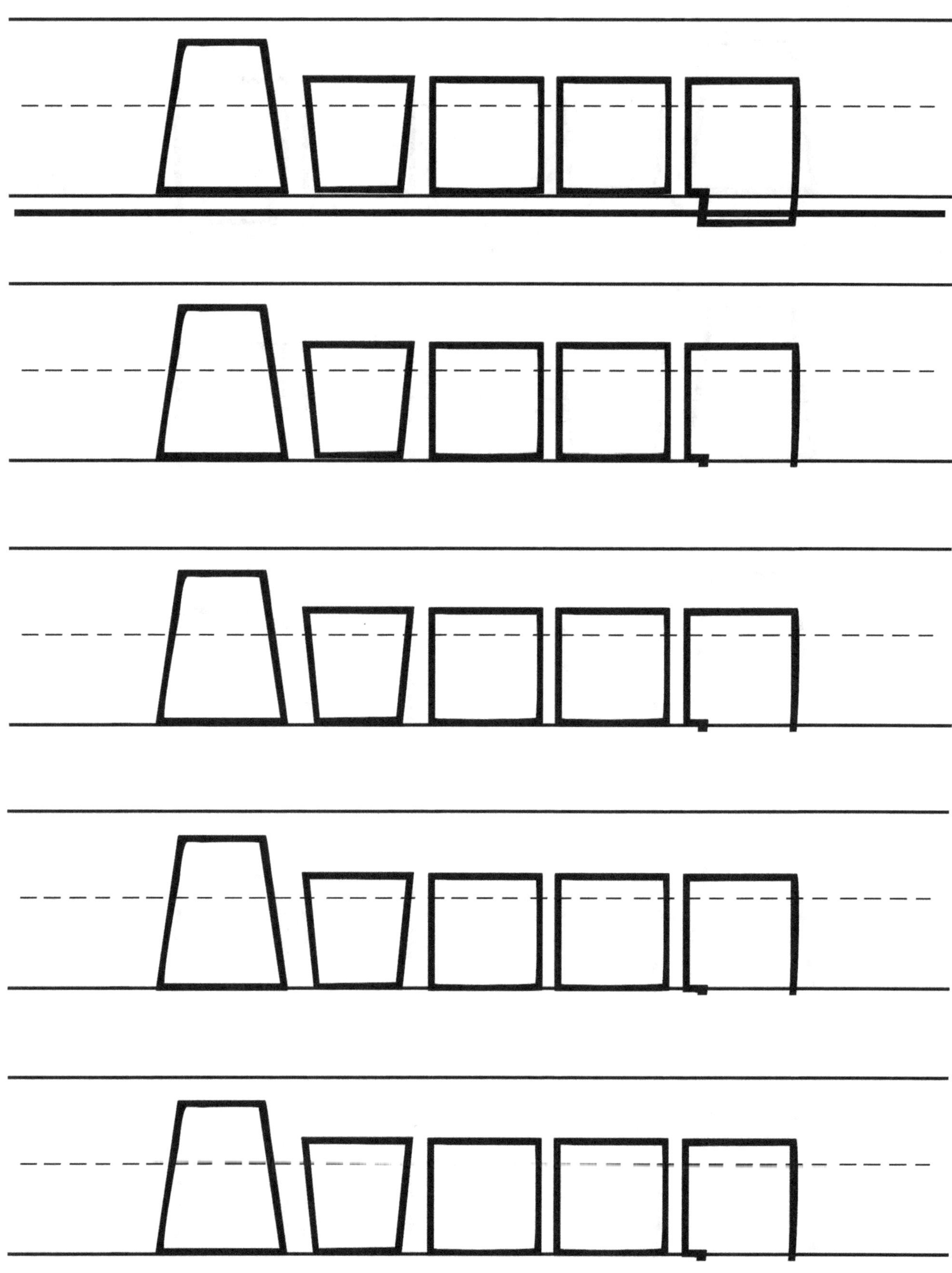

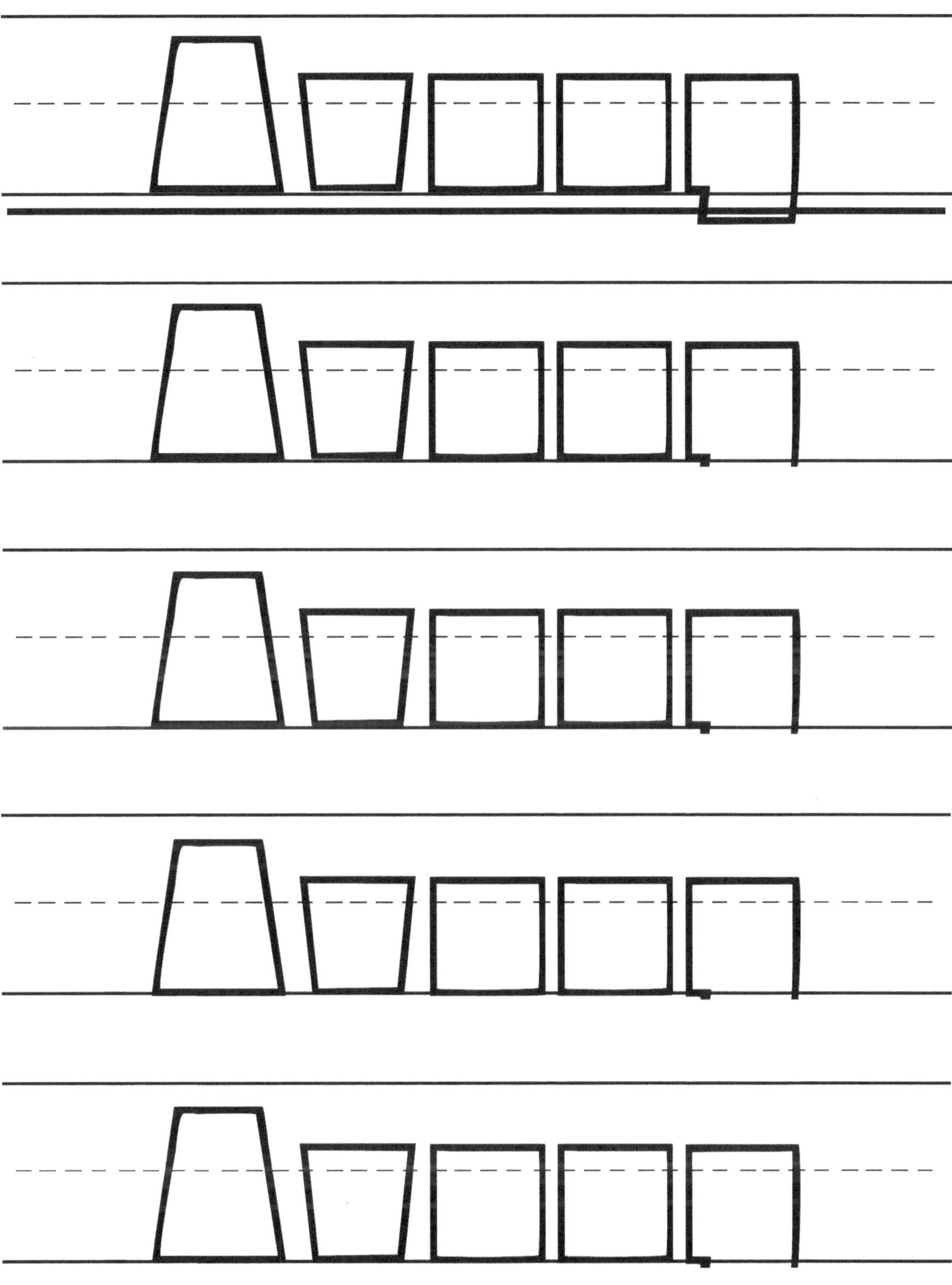

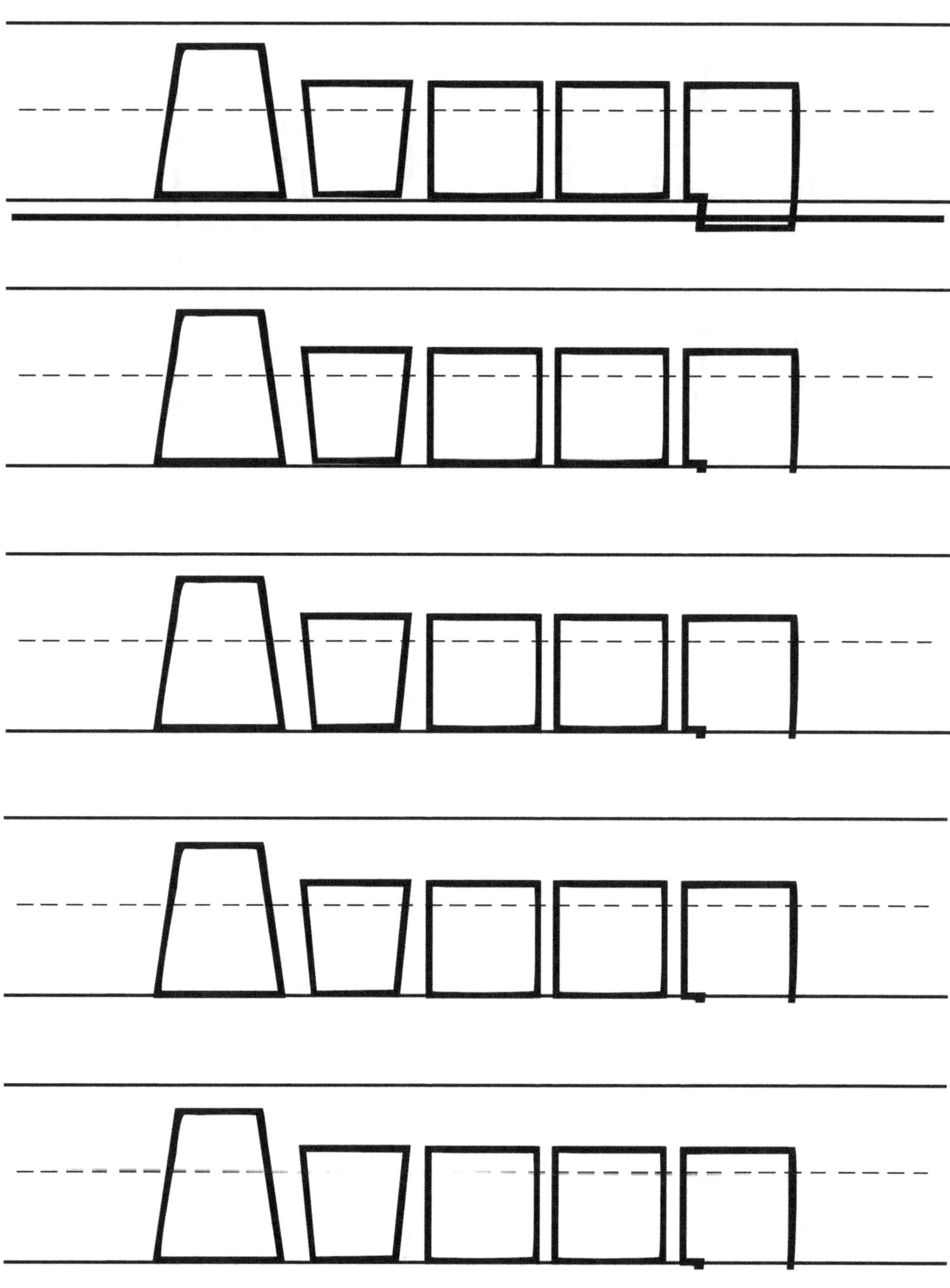

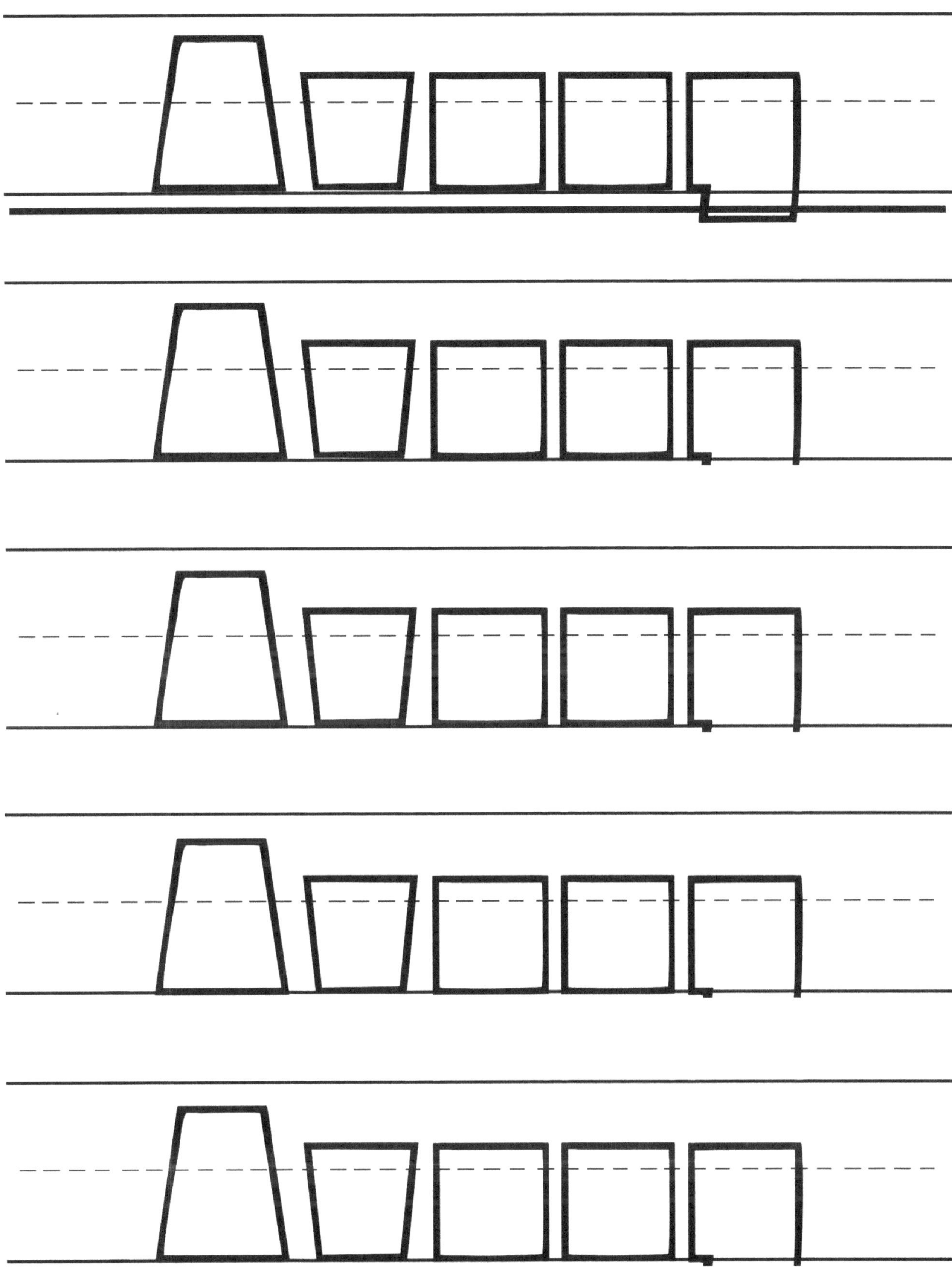

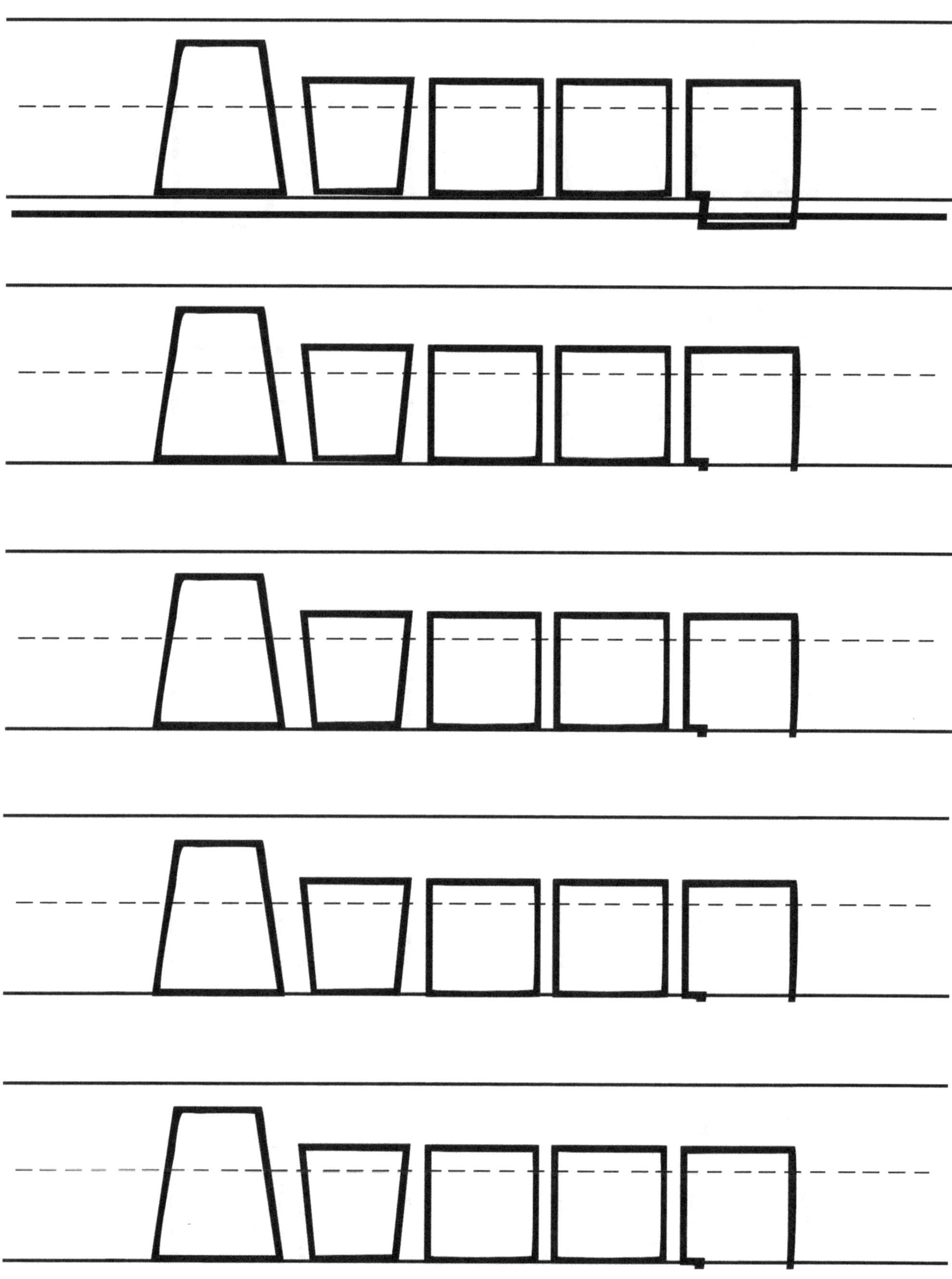

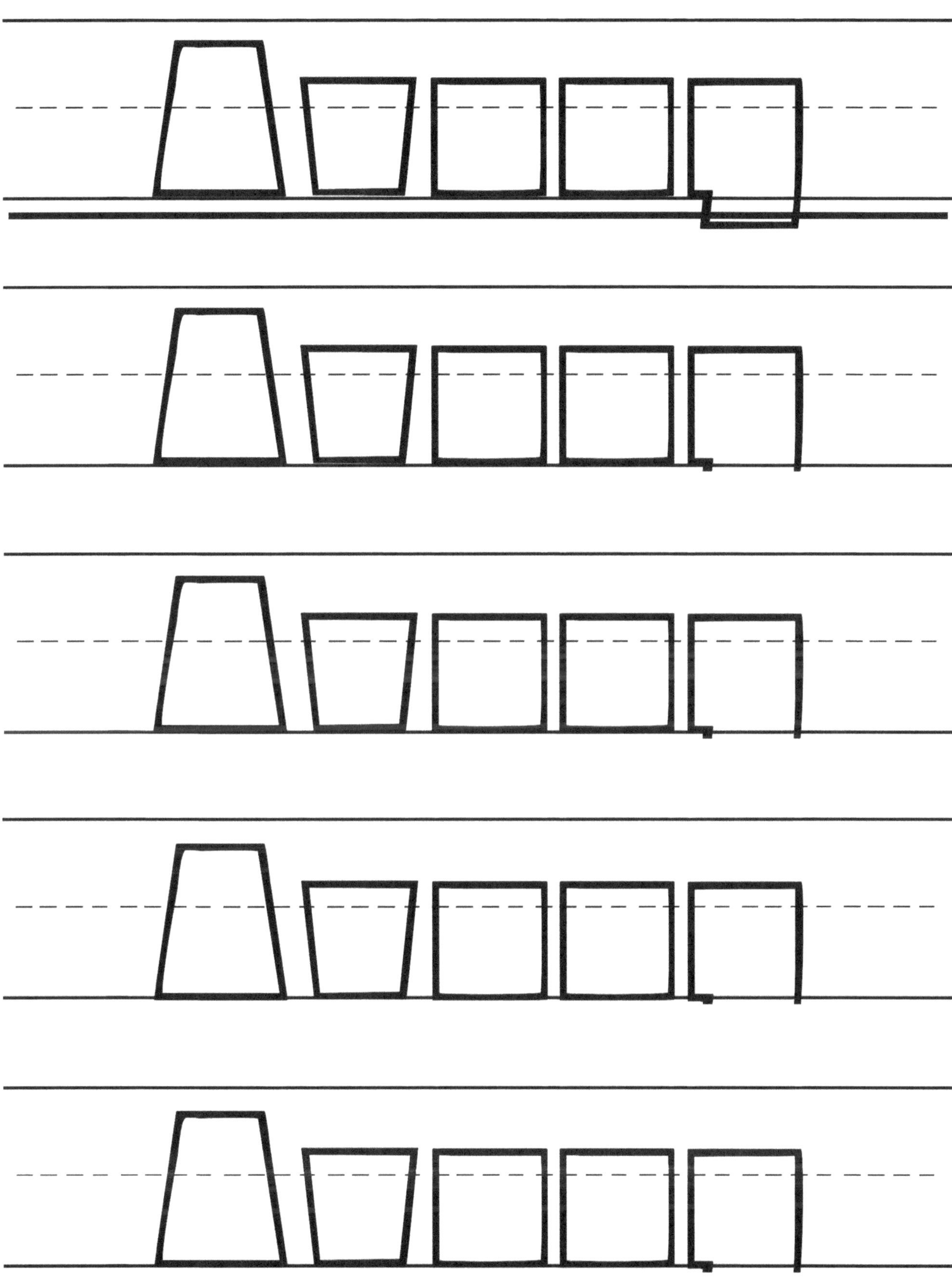

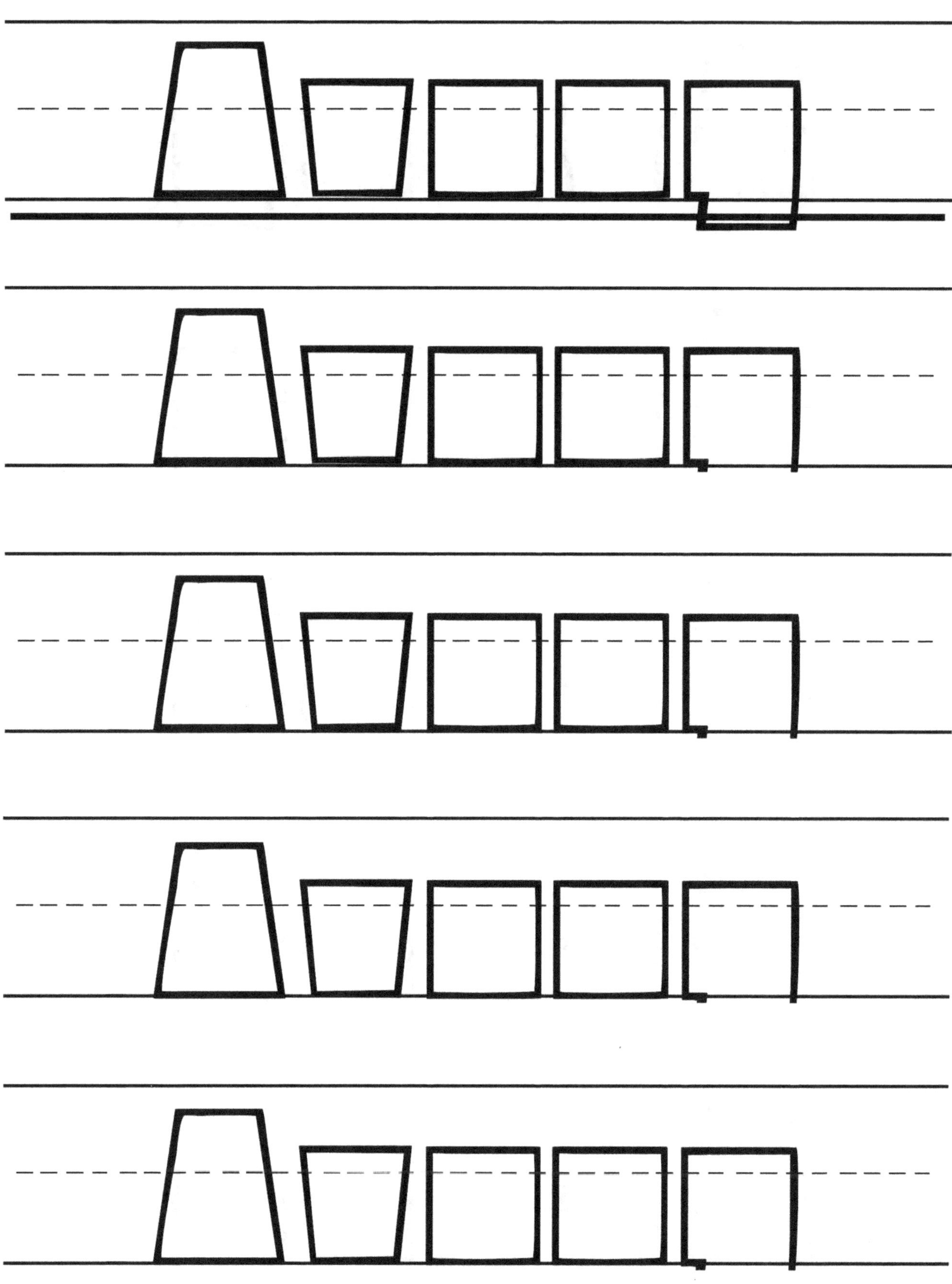

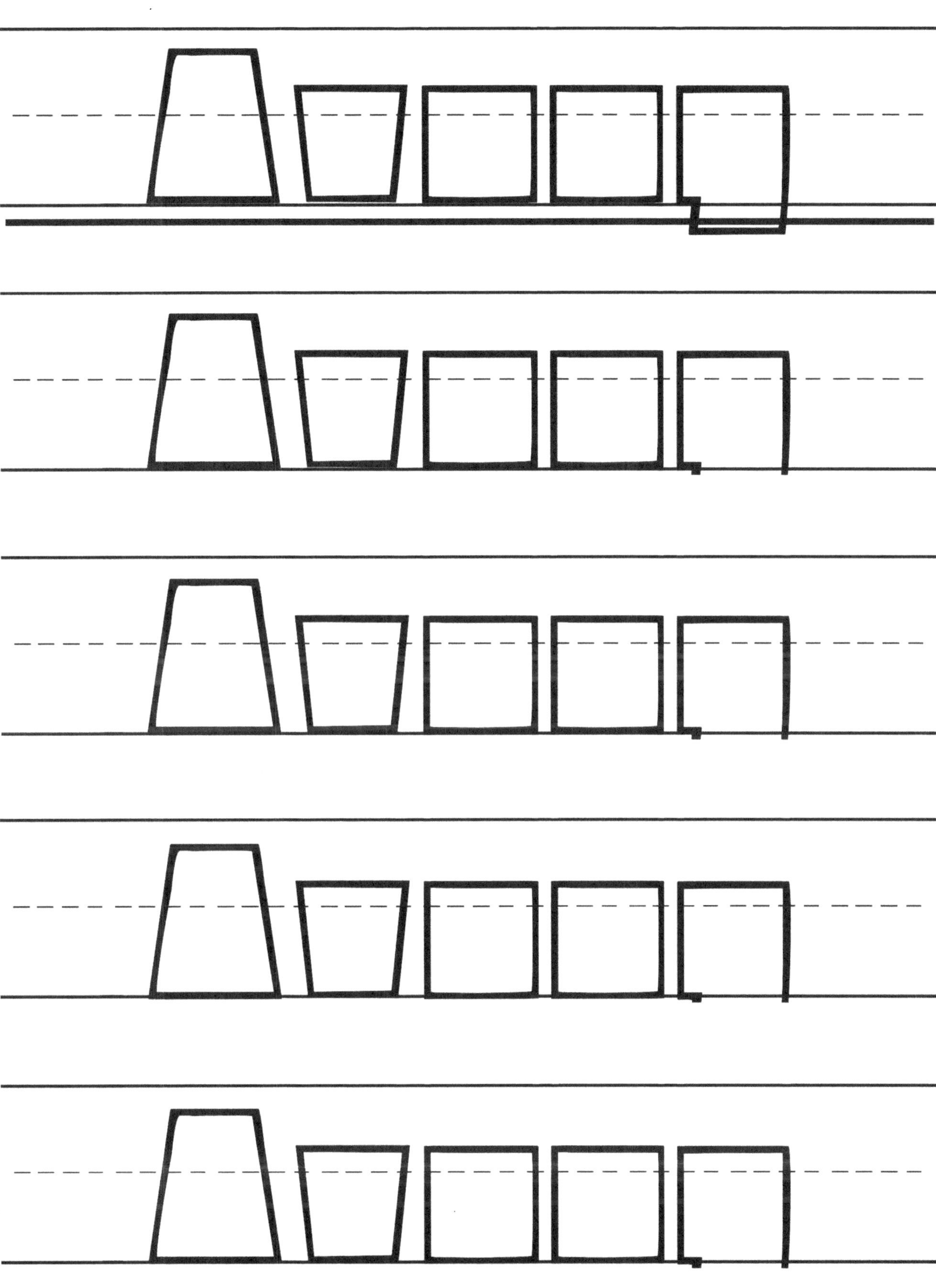

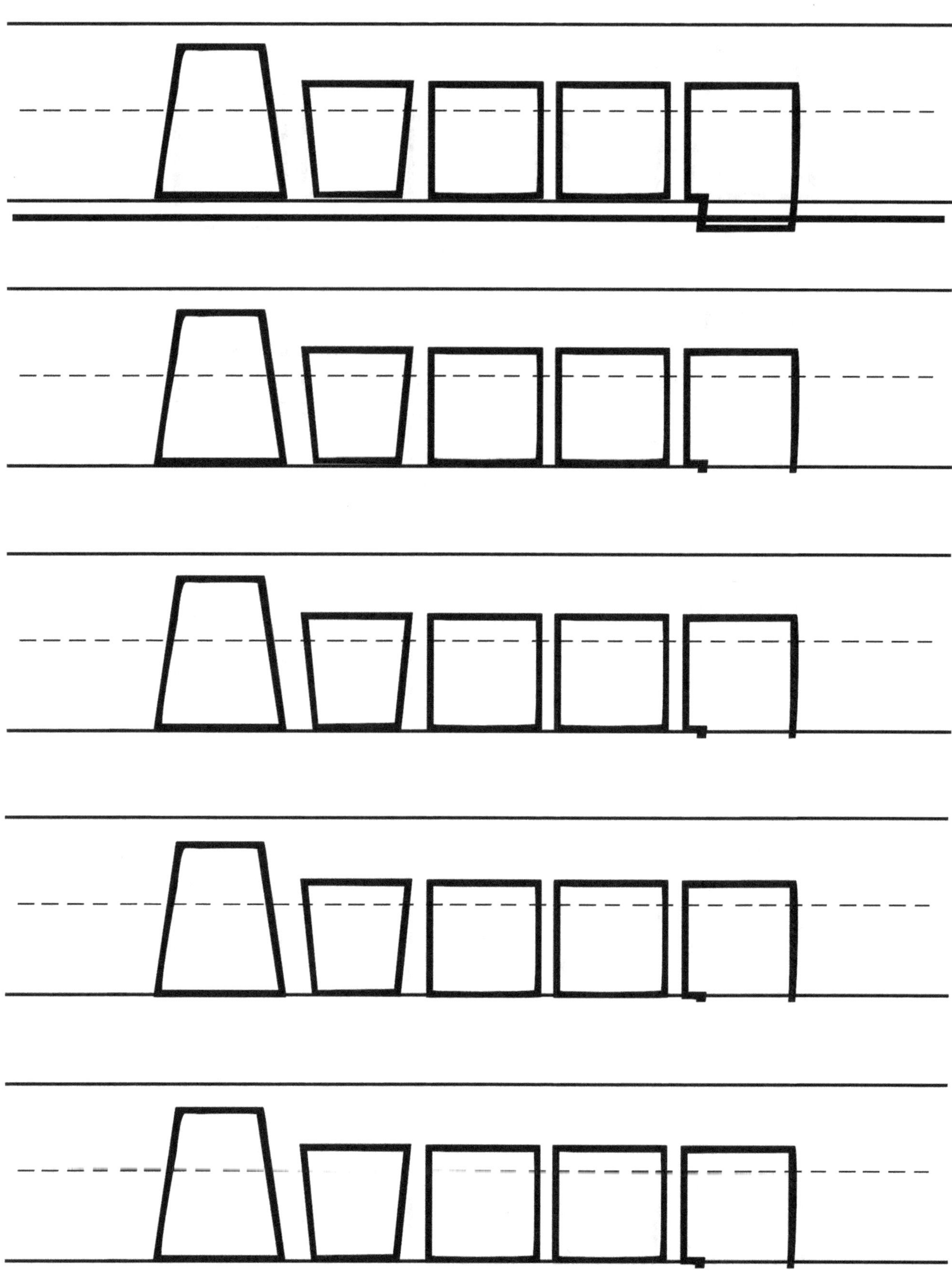

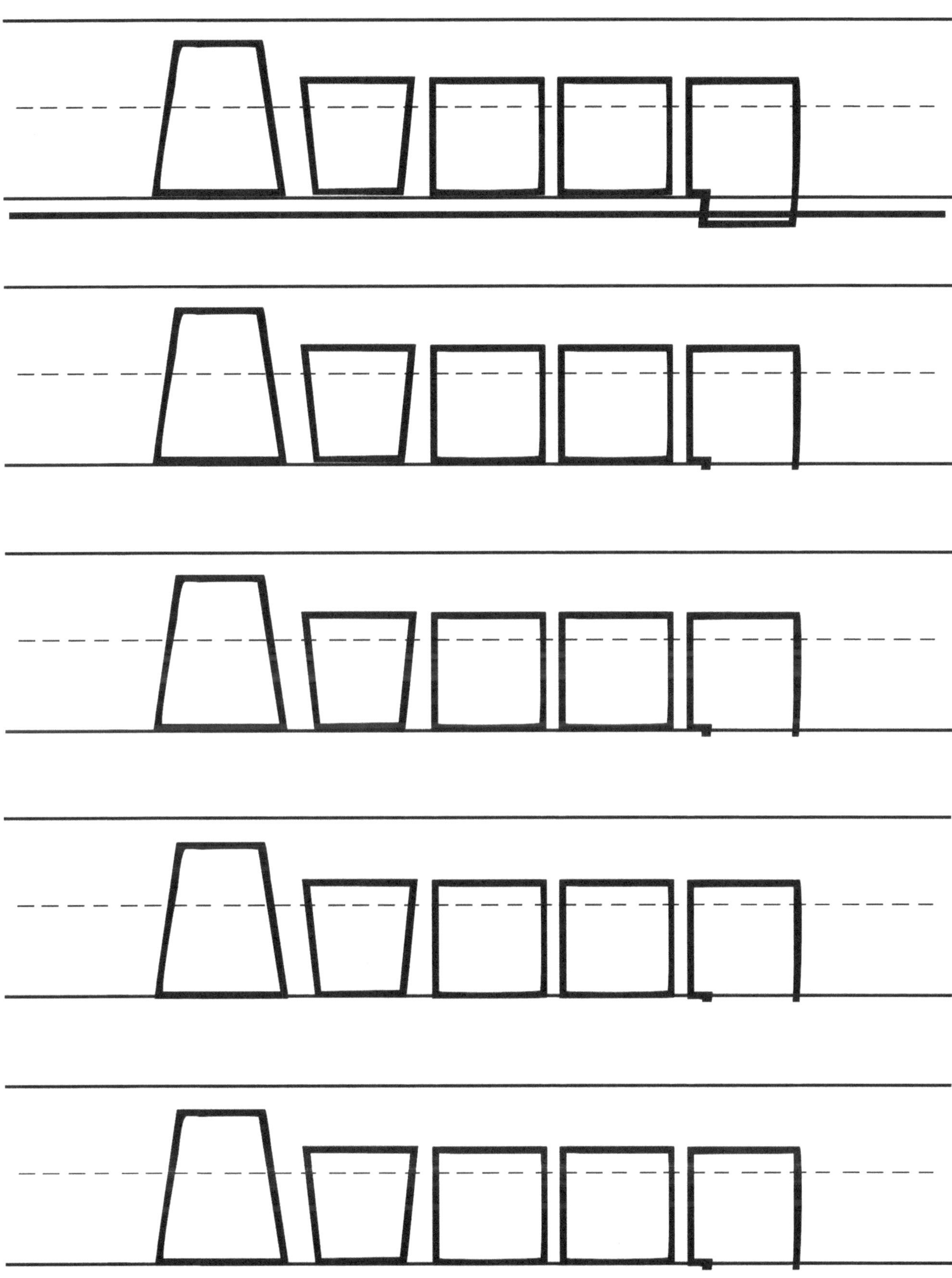

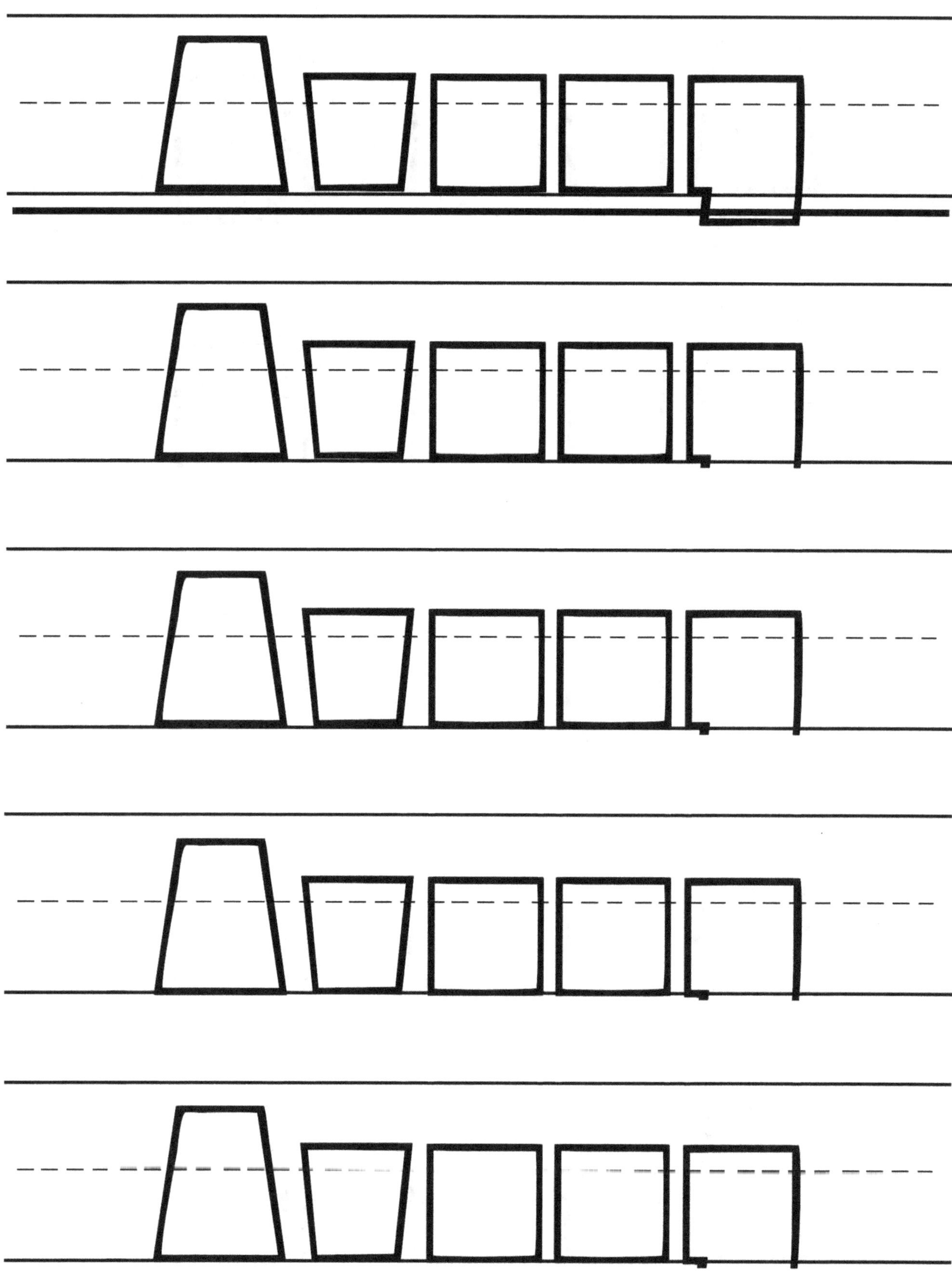

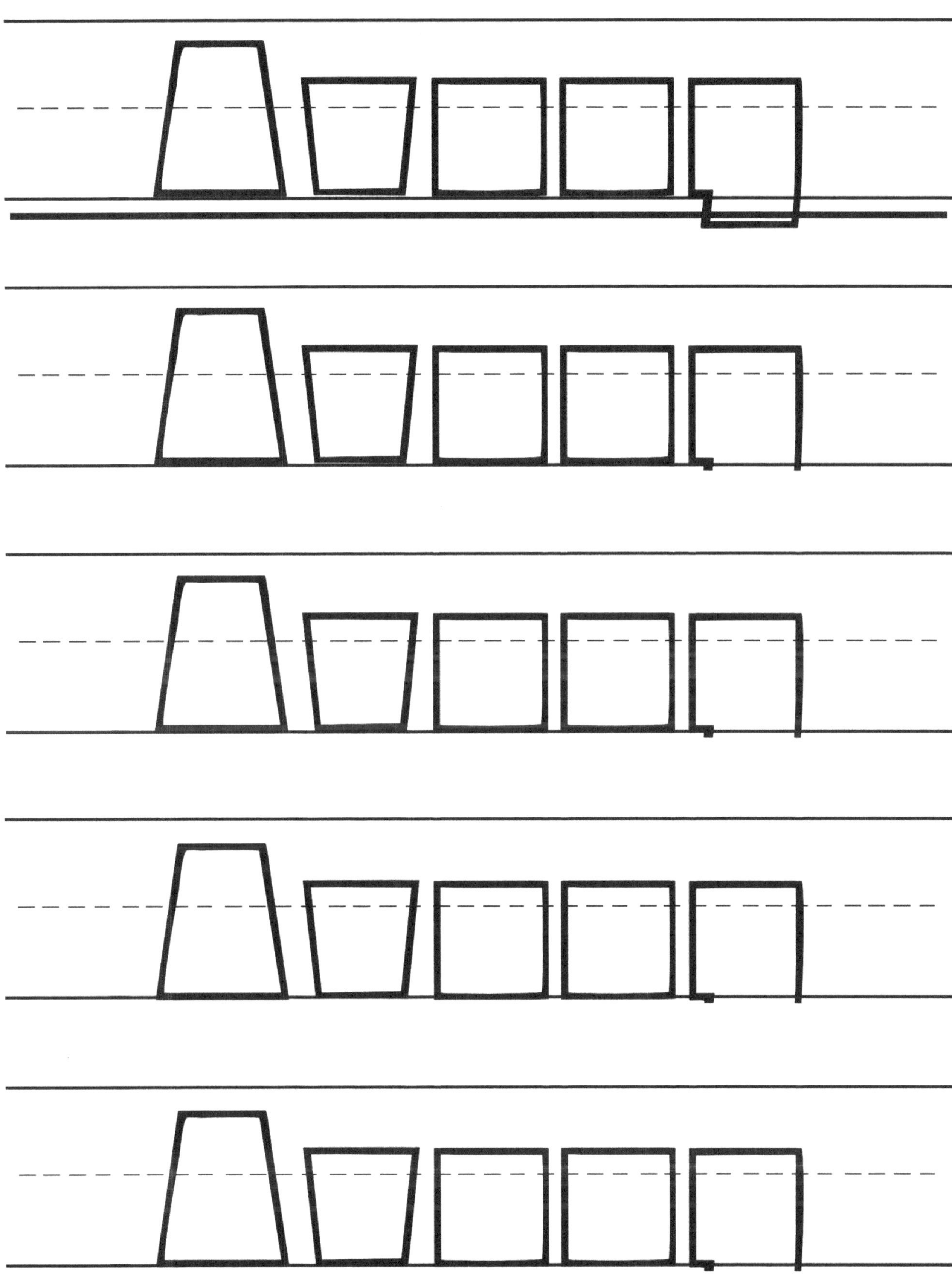

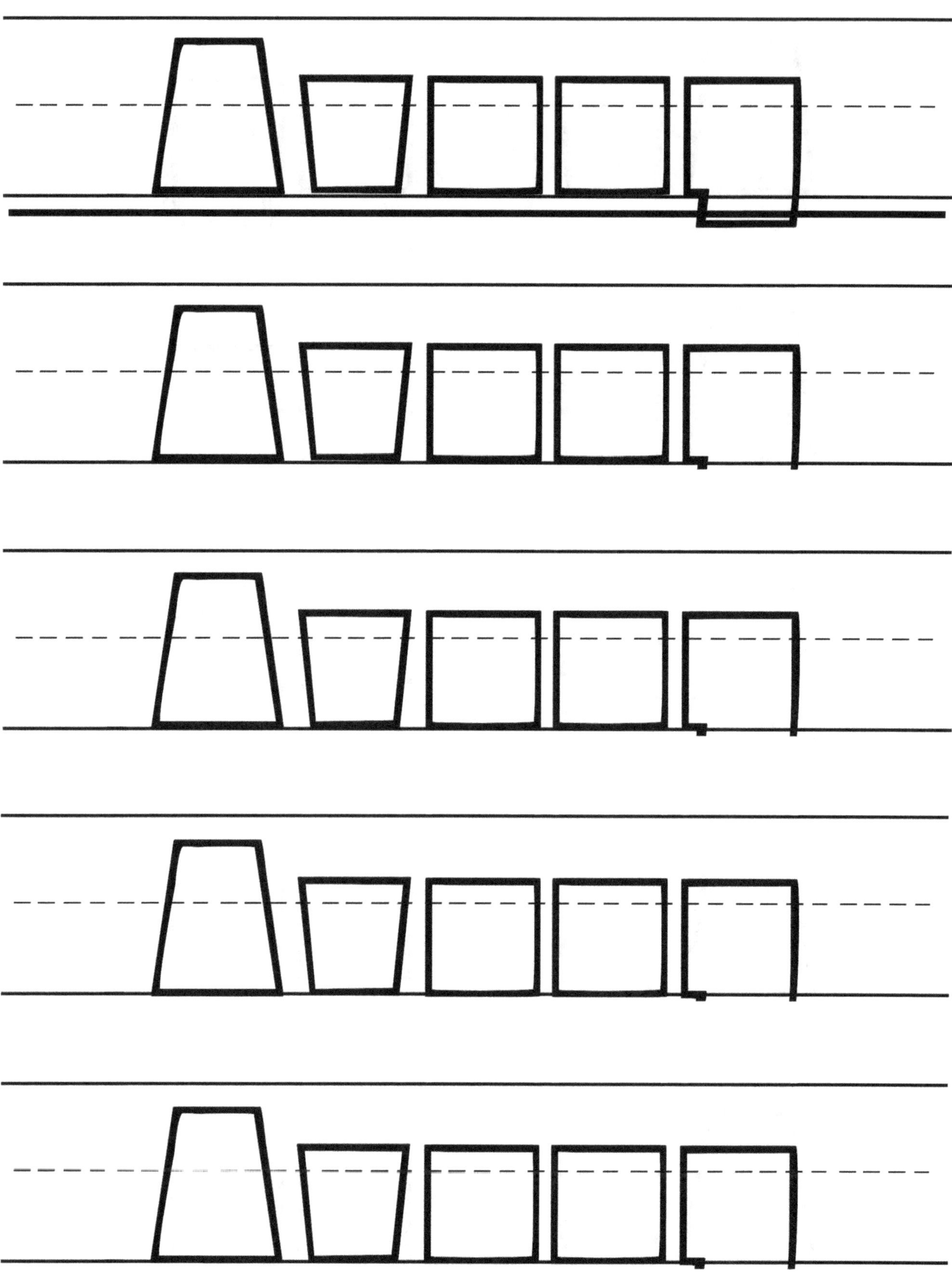

Avery

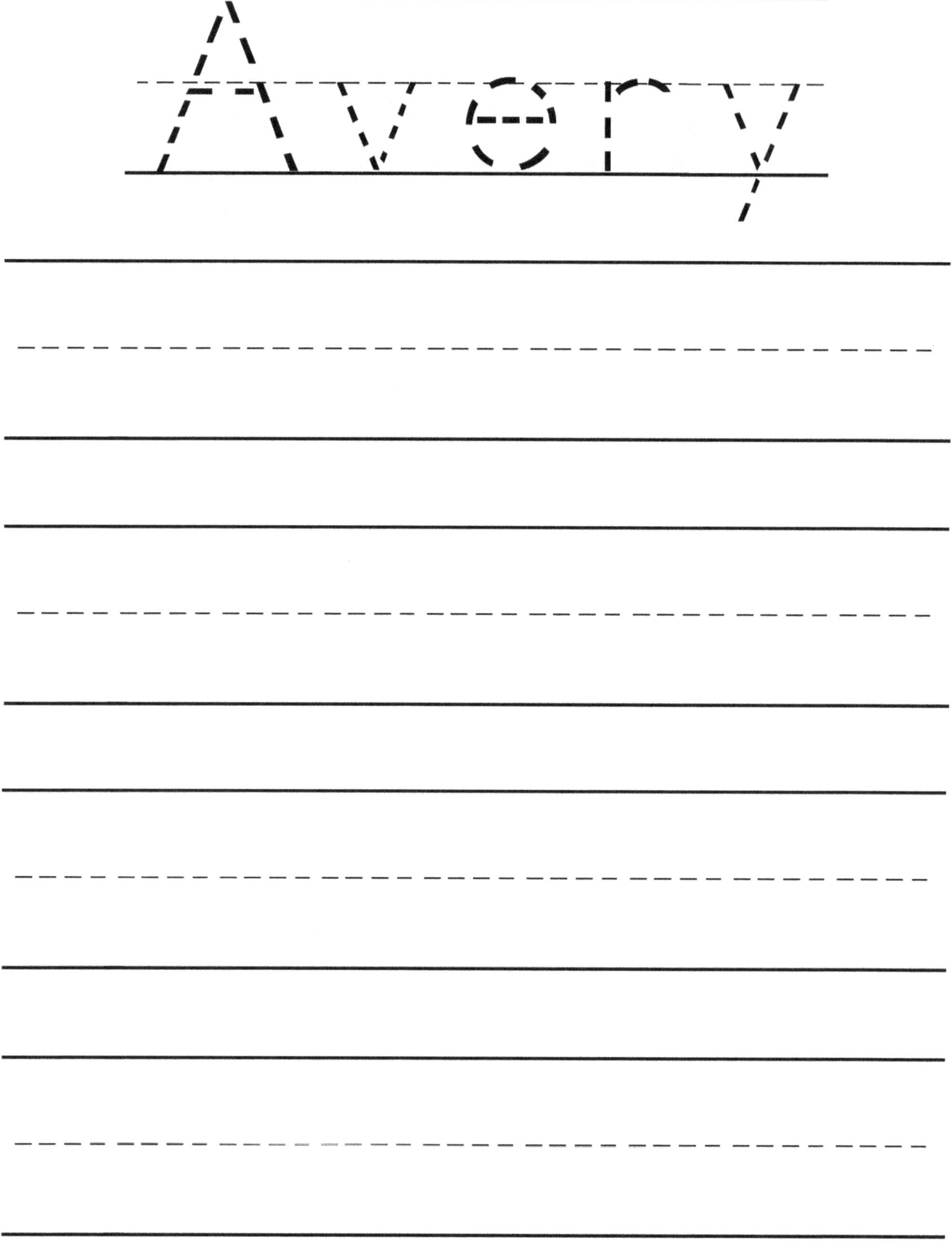

Avery

Avery

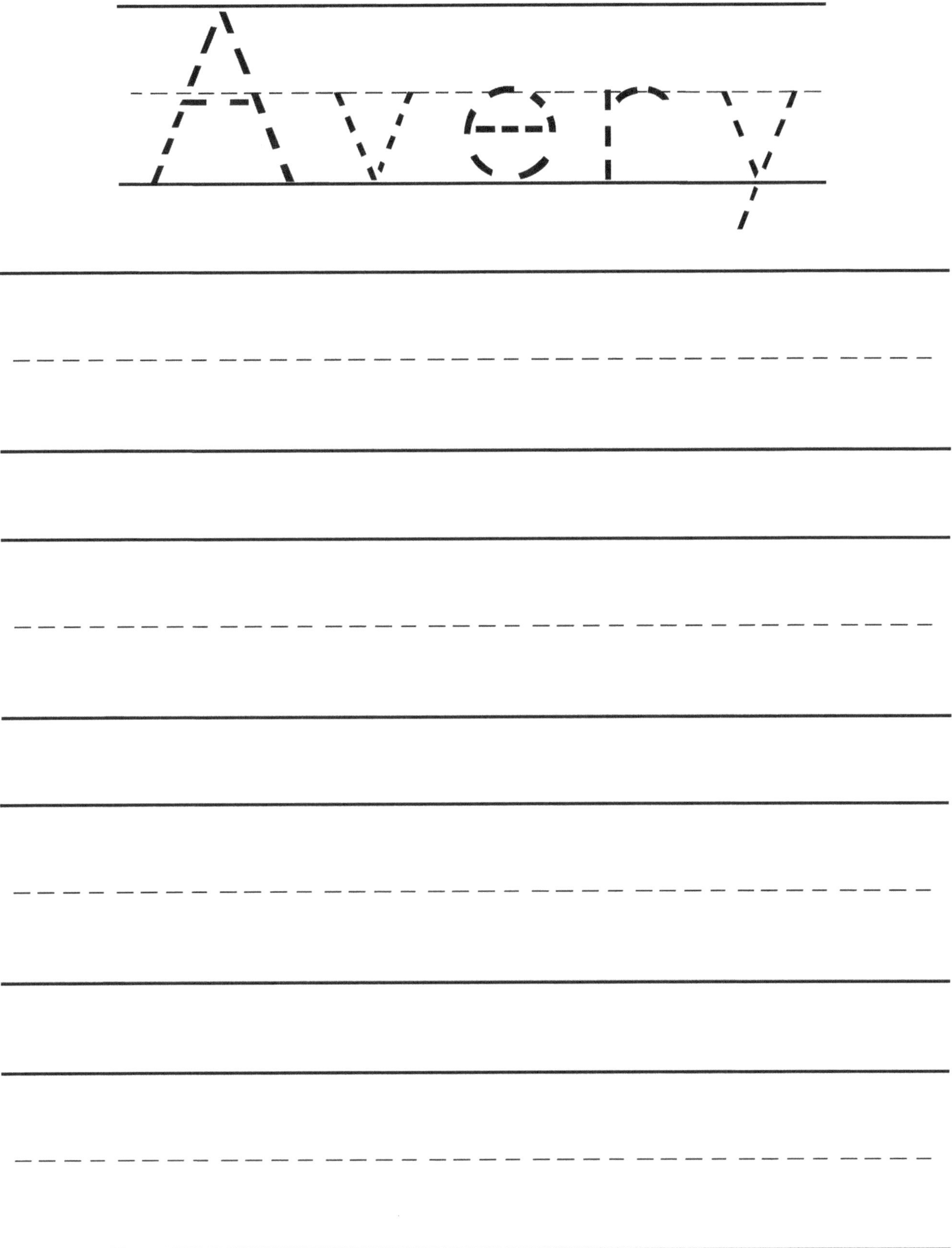
Avery

Avery

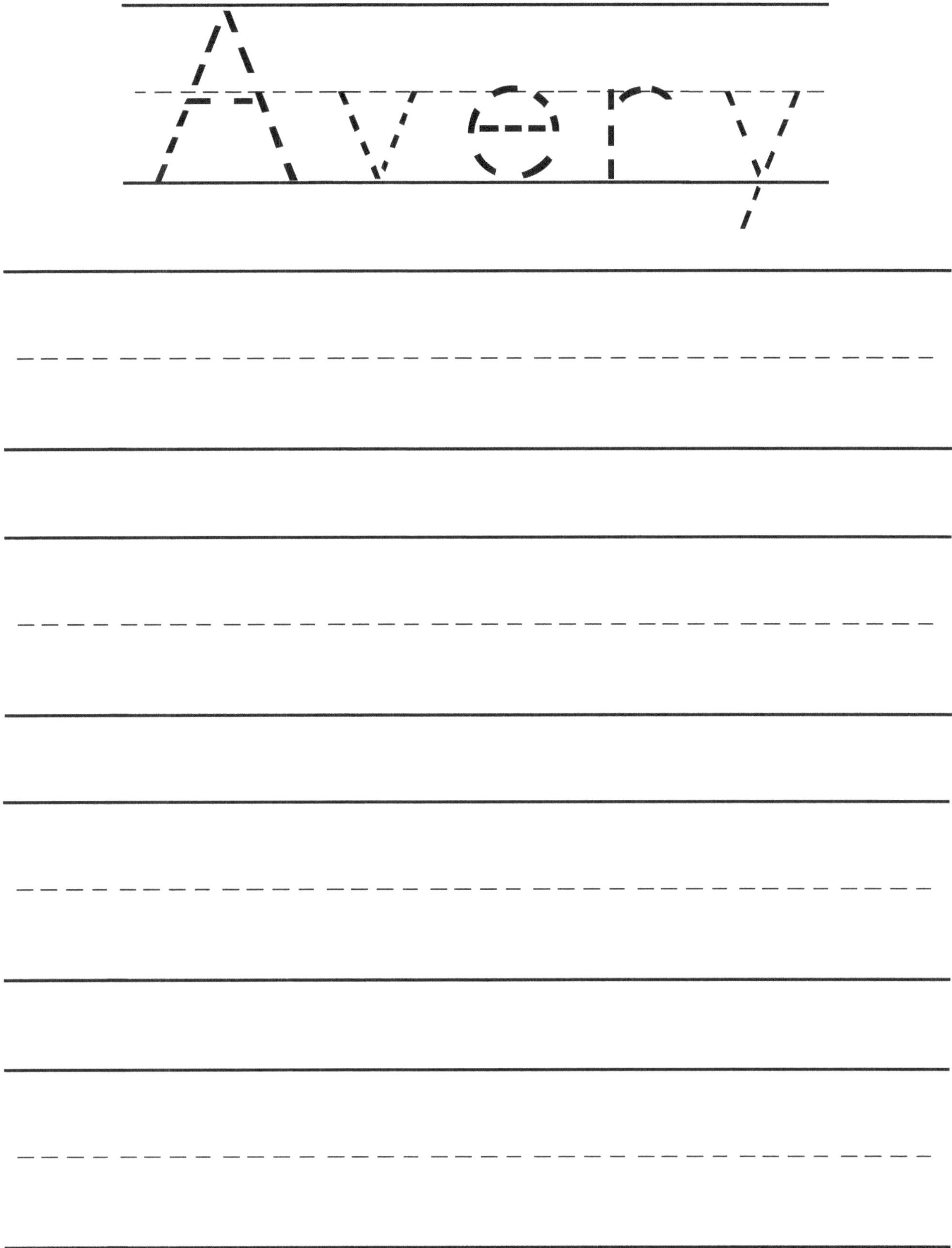
Avery

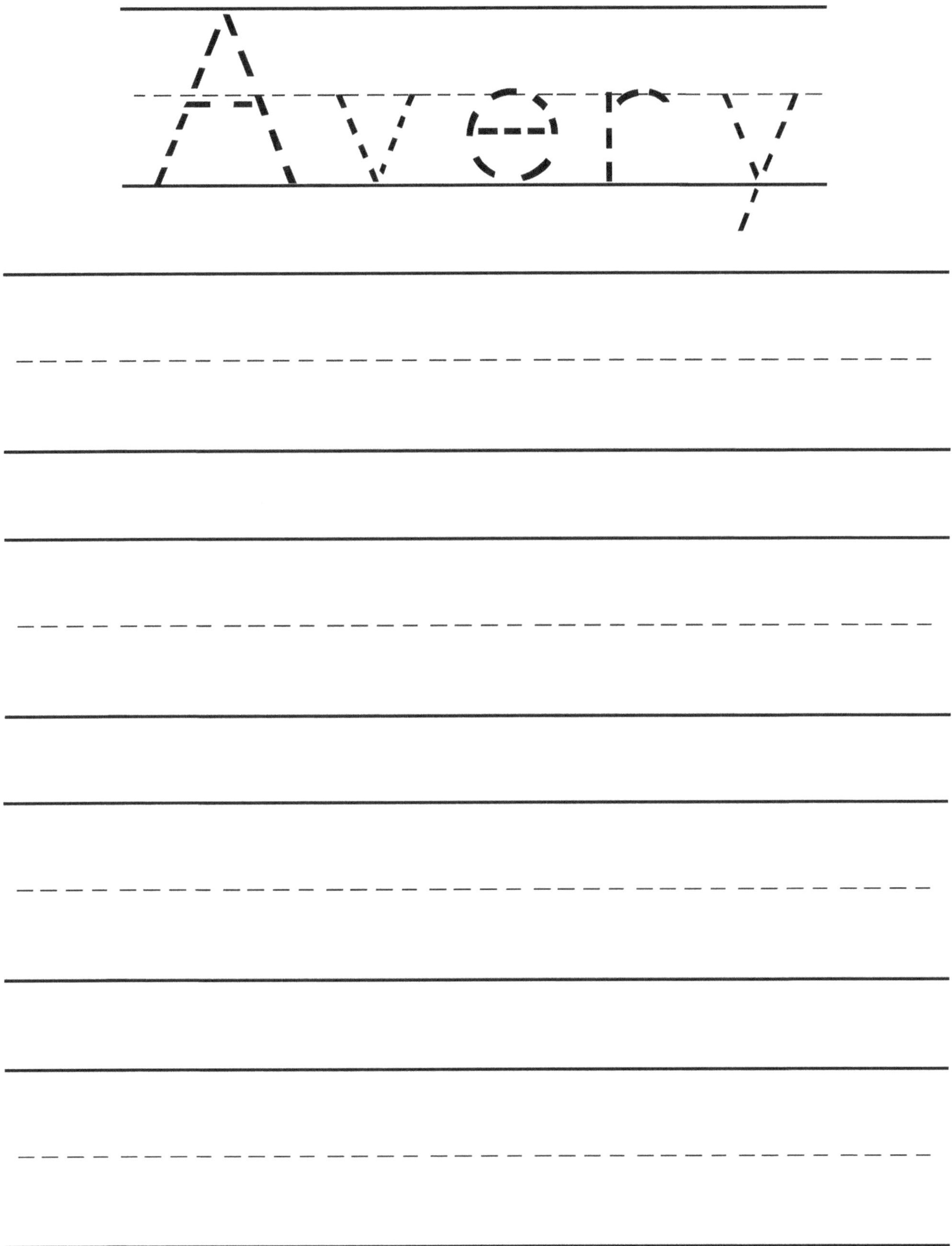

Avery

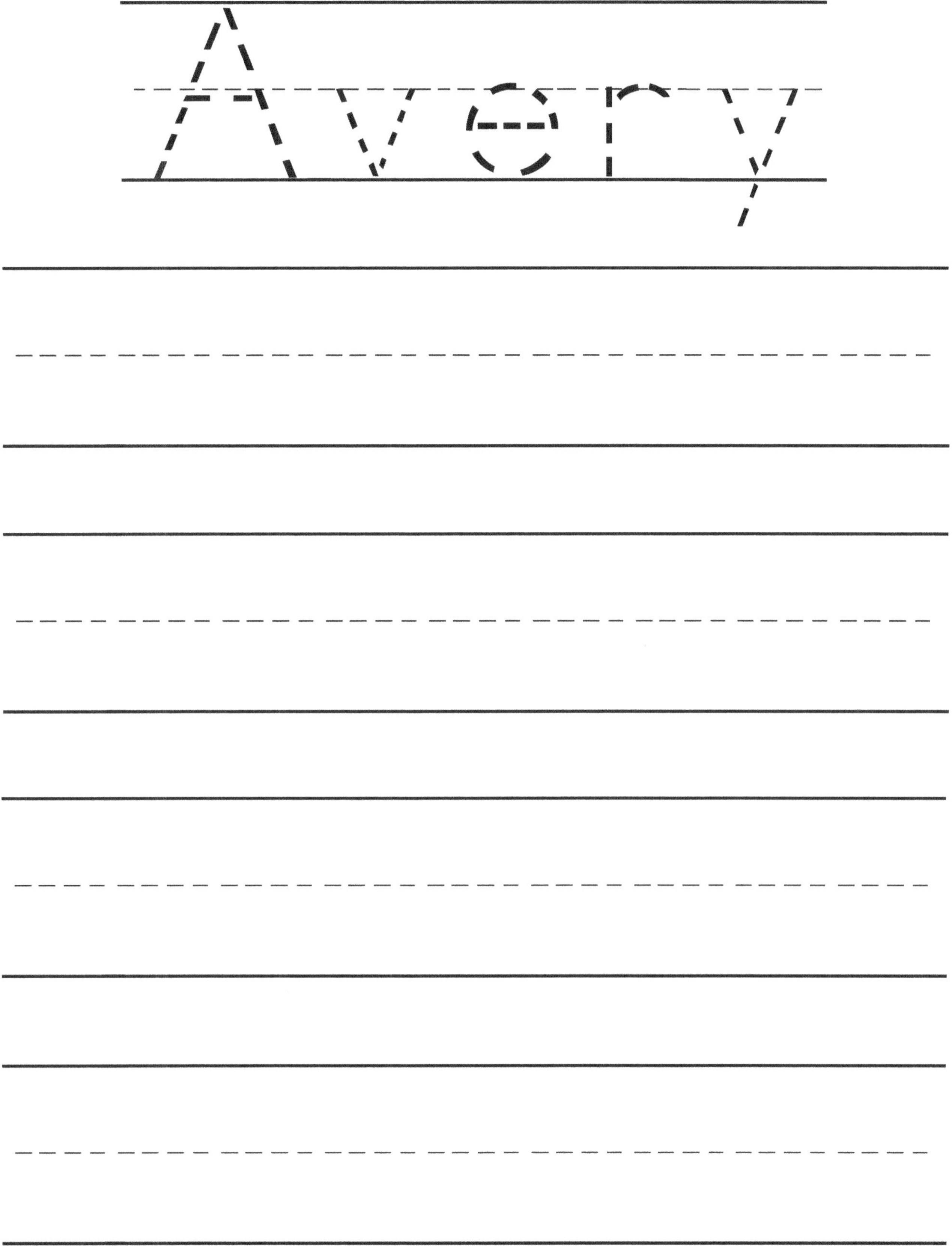
Avery

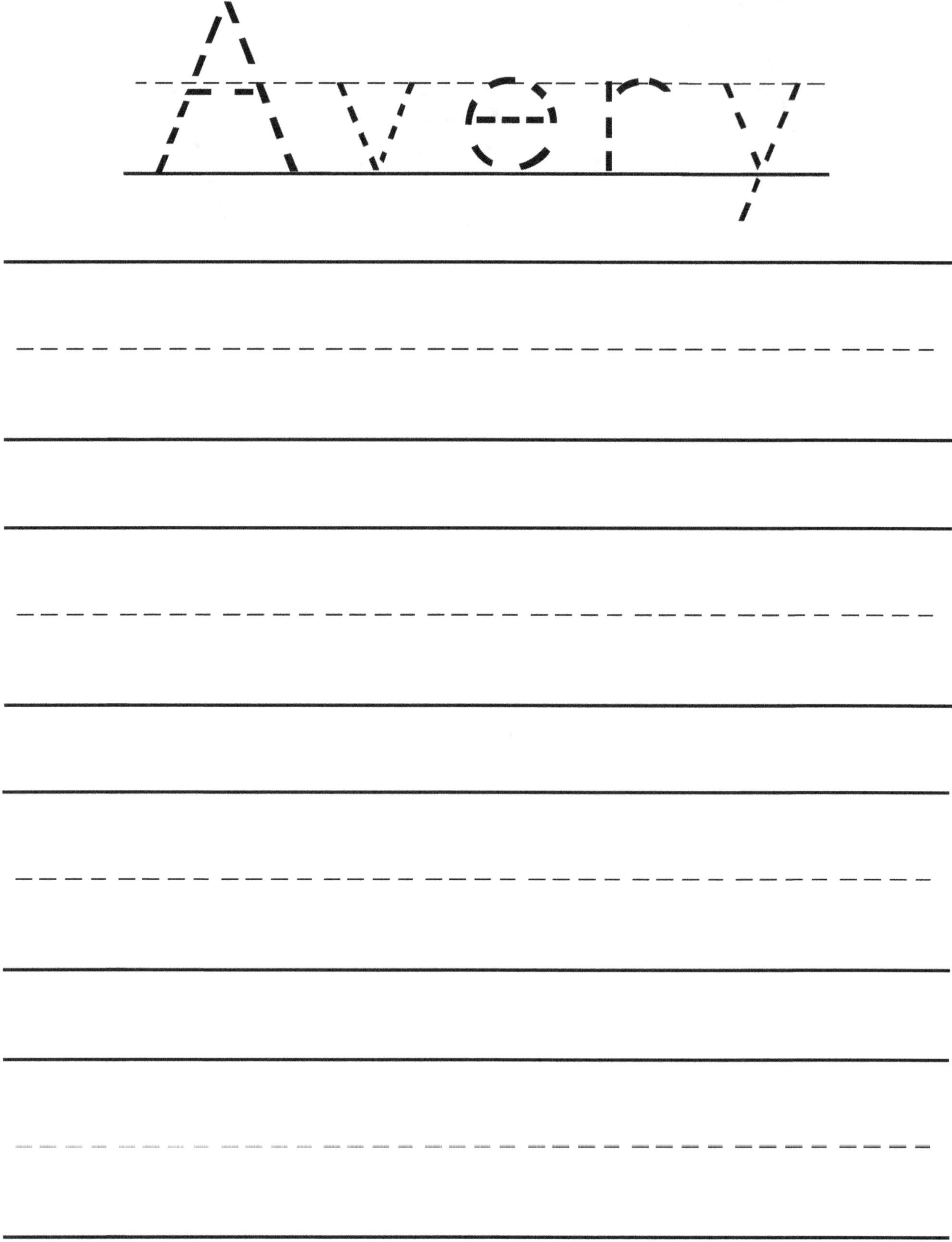

Avery

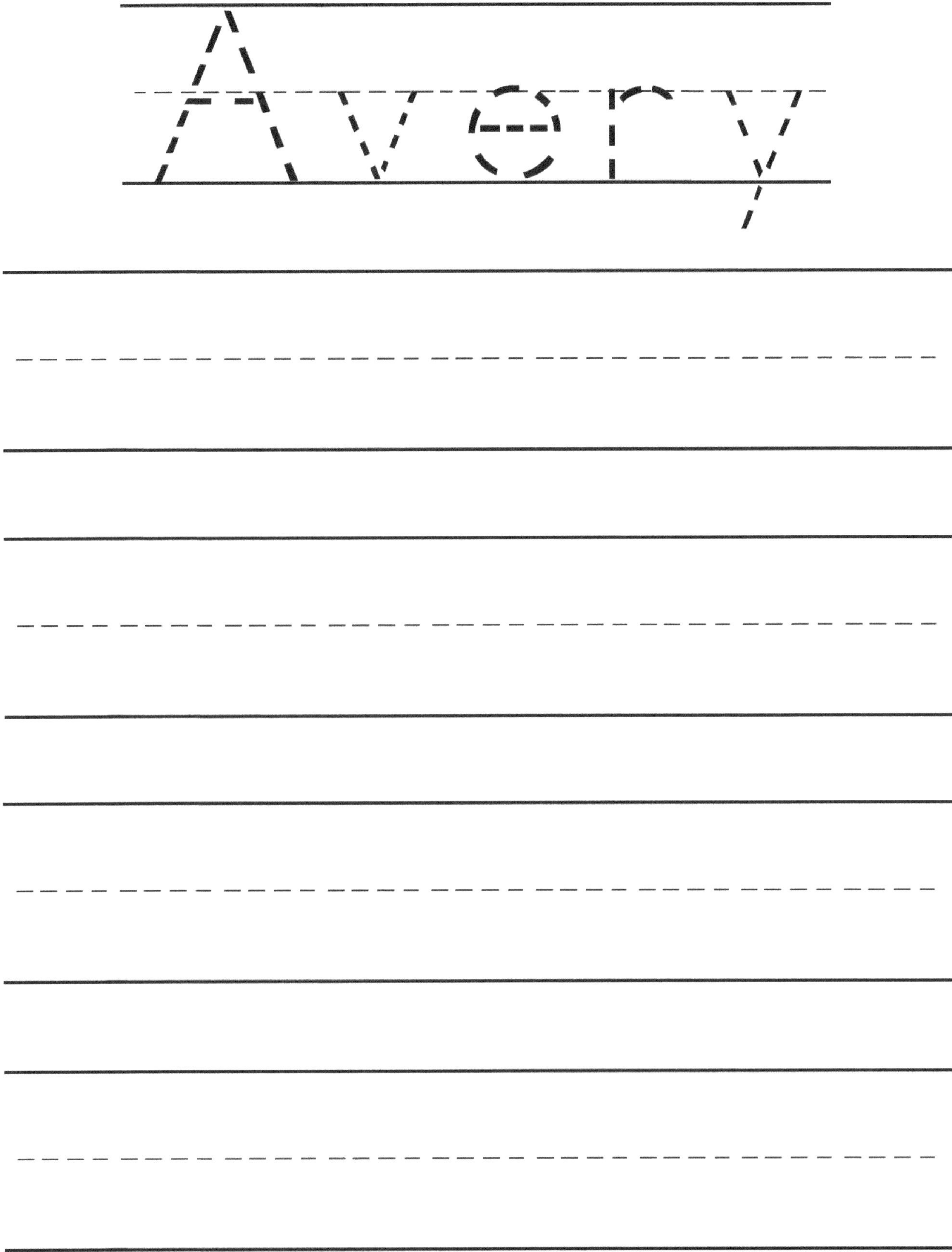
Avery

Avery

Avery

Avery

Avery

Avery

Avery

Avery

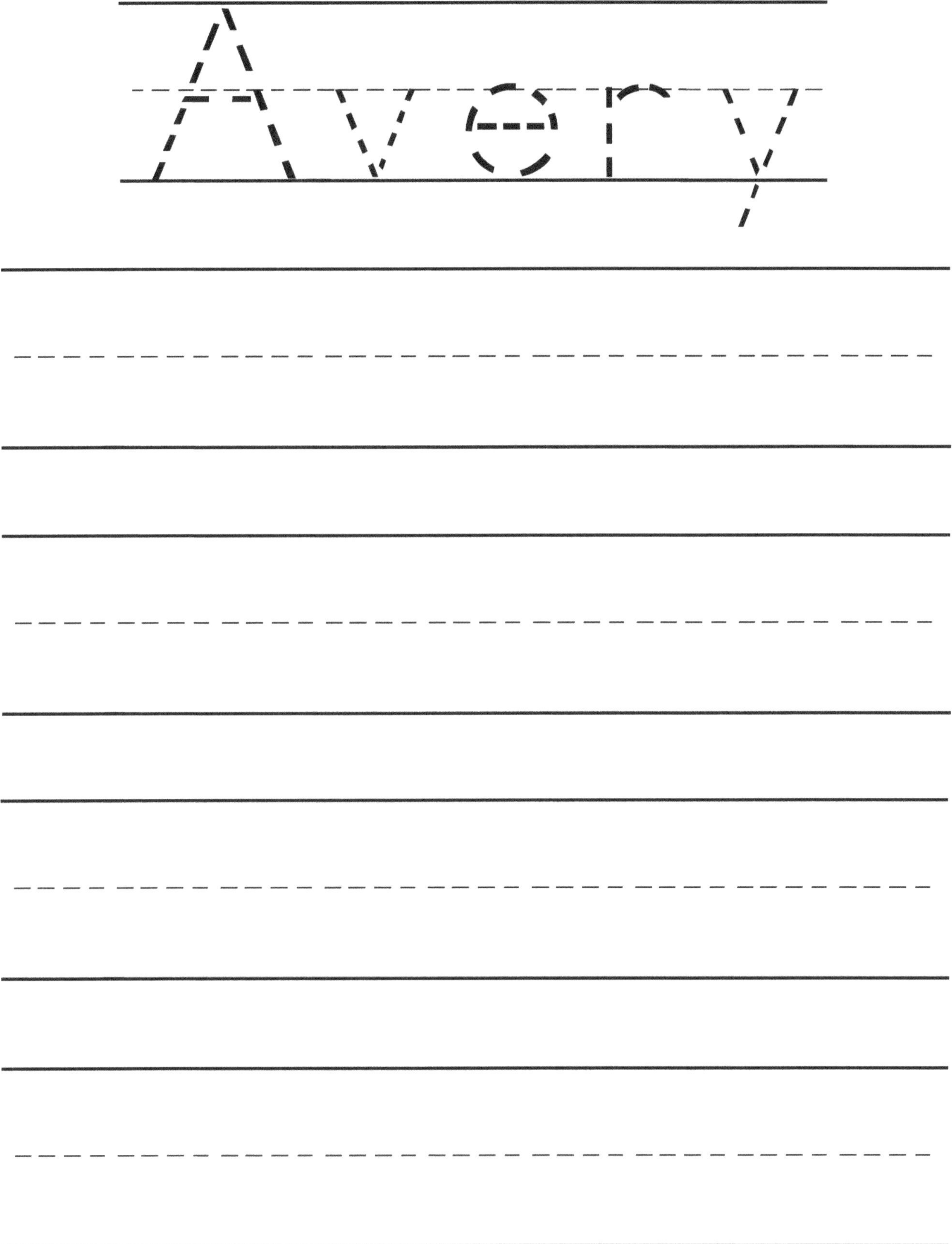

Avery

Avery

Avery

Avery

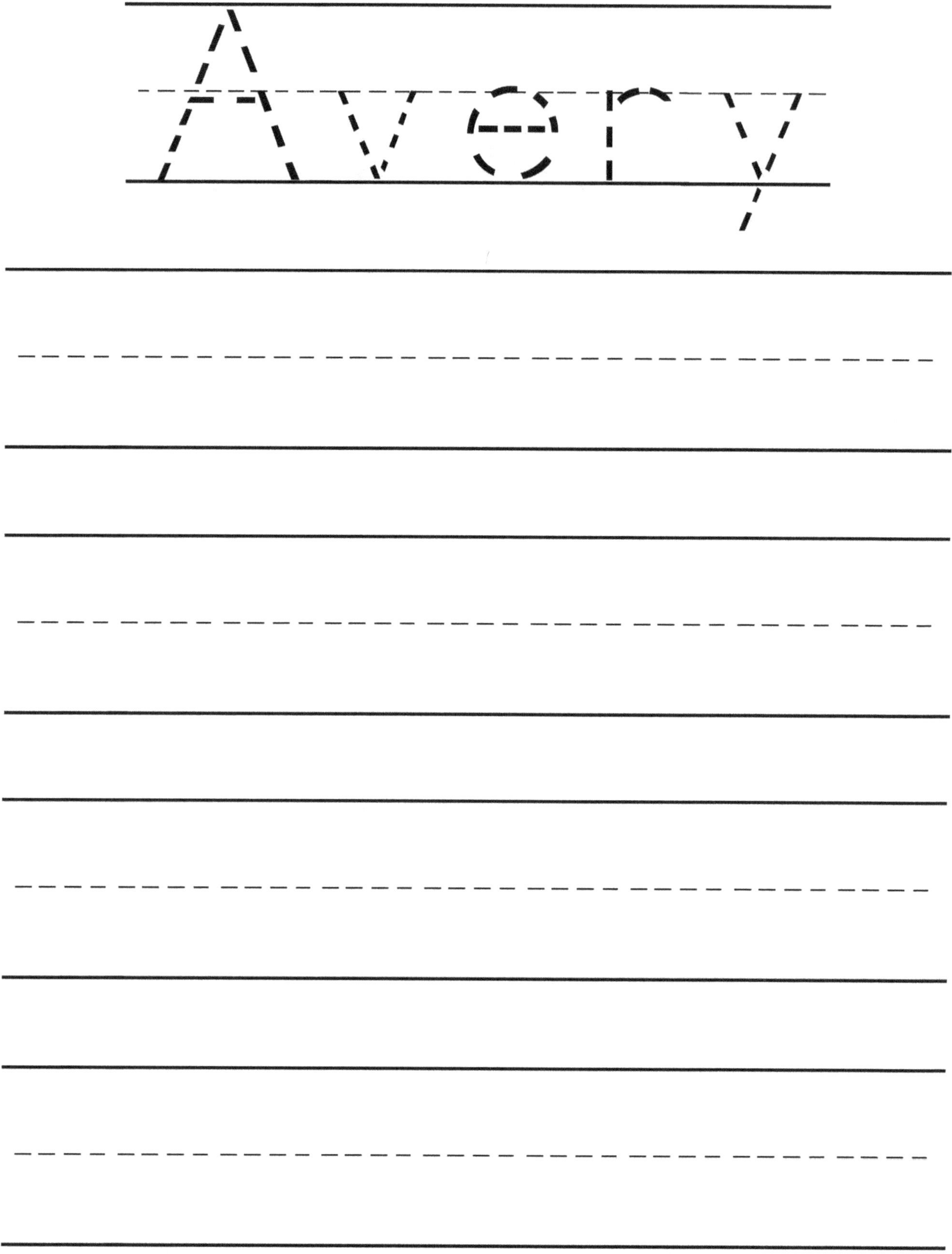

Avery

Avery

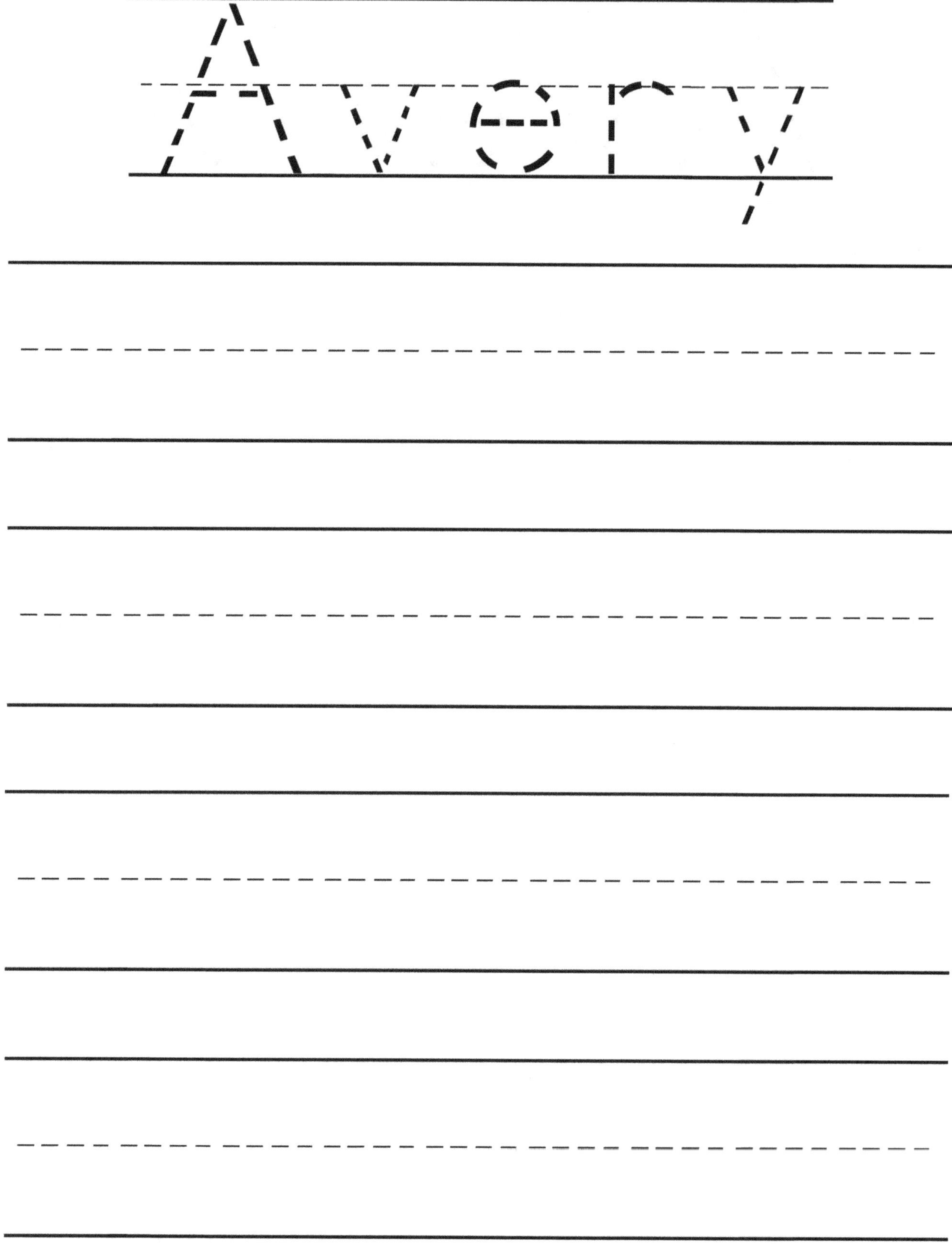

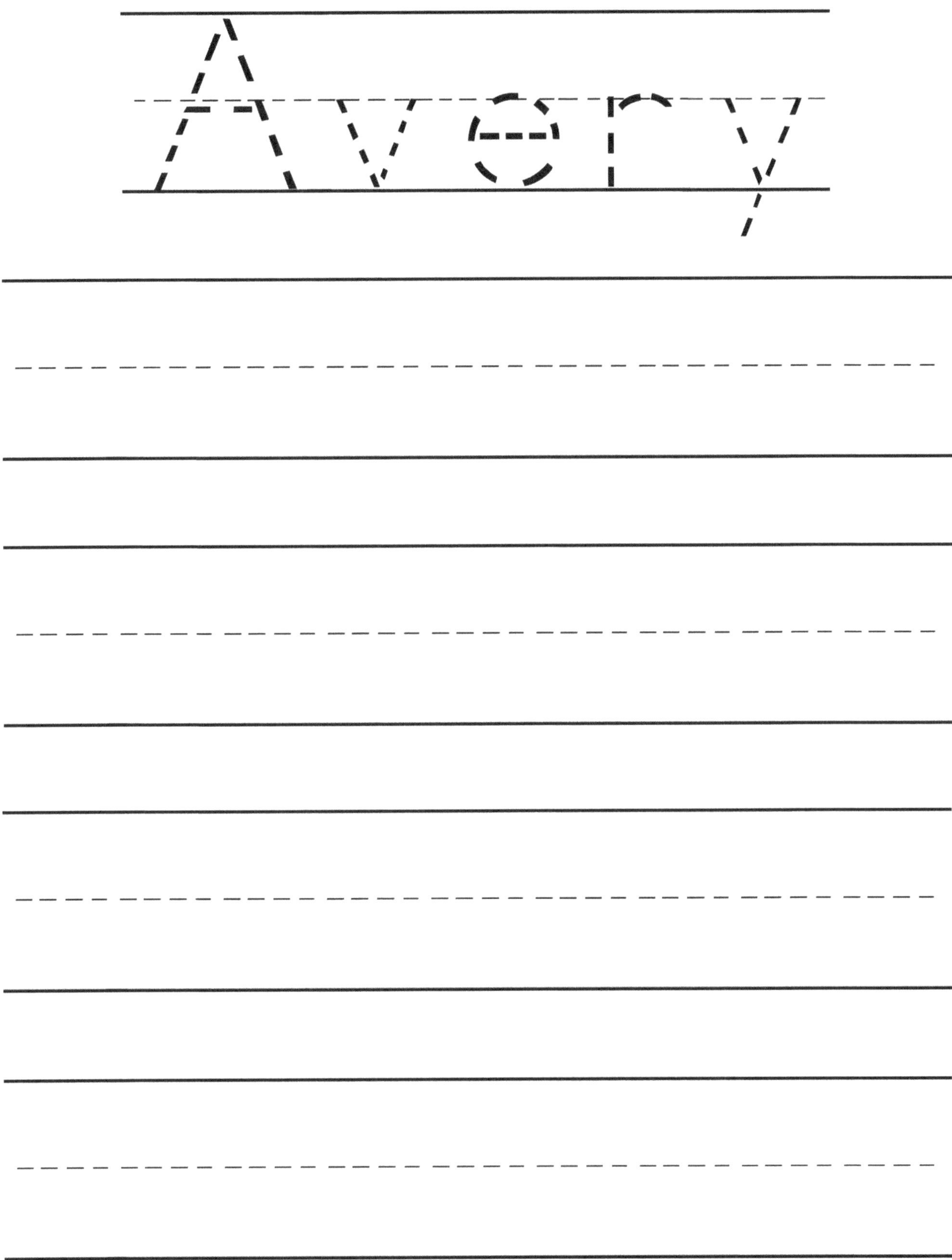

Avery

Avery

Avery

Avery

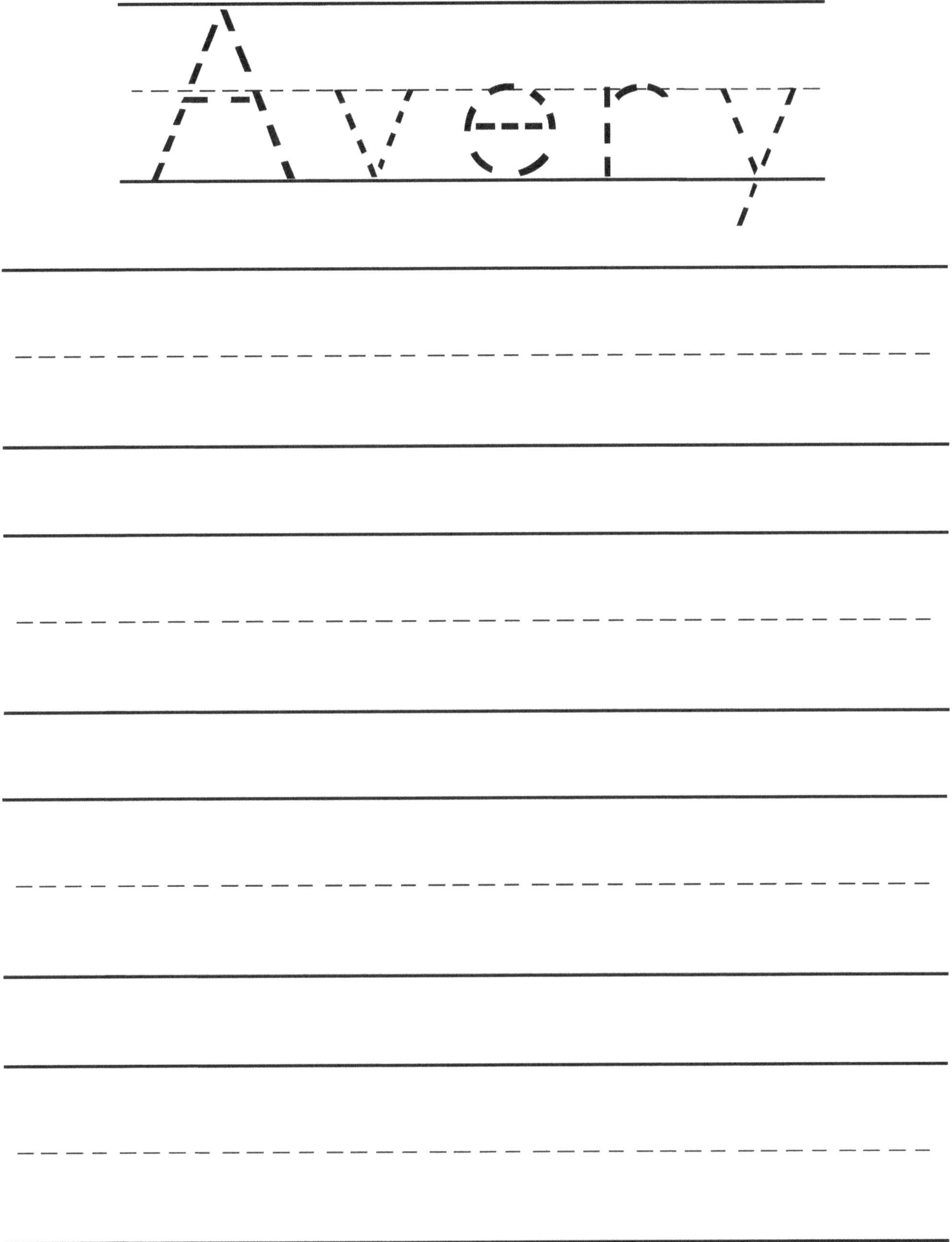
Avery

Avery

Avery

Avery

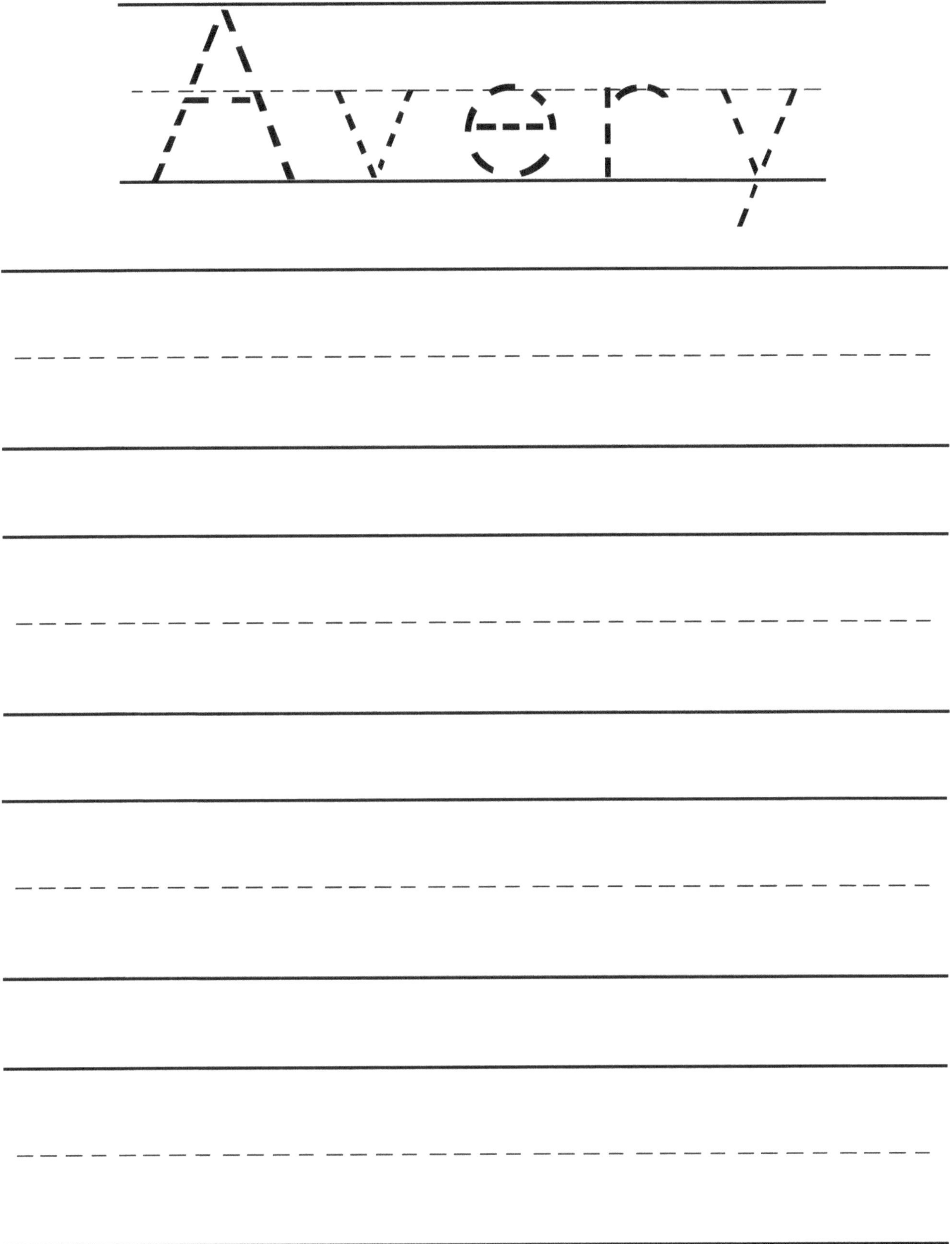
Avery

Avery

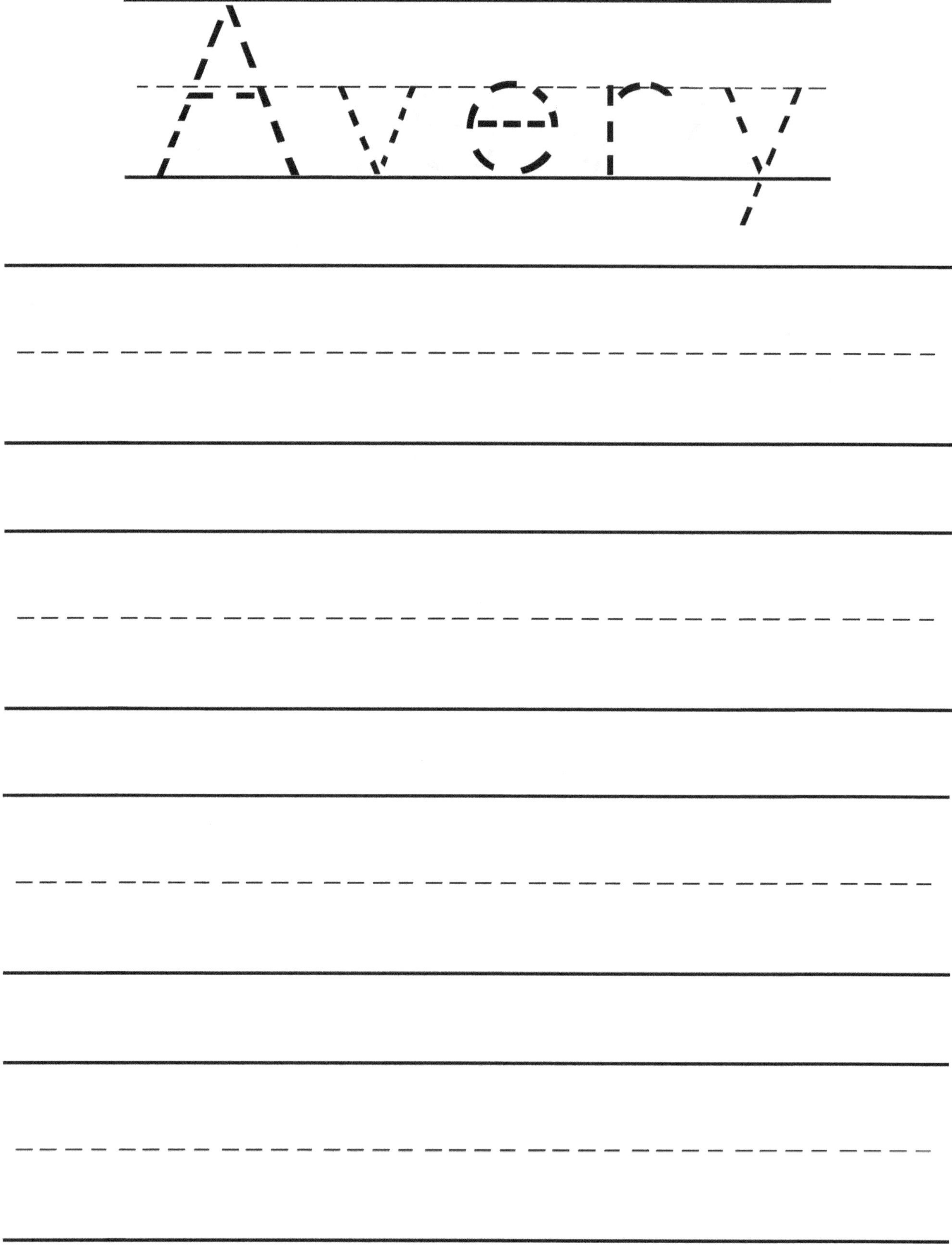
Avery

Avery

Avery

Avery

Avery

www.ingramcontent.com/pod-product-compliance
Lightning Source LLC
Chambersburg PA
CBHW080305030726
47593CB00009B/2643